The Compliance Edge

HOW DISRUPTIVE ENTREPRENEURS WIN IN REGULATED MARKETS

LEE J BRYAN

Re^think

First published in Great Britain in 2026
by Rethink Press (www.rethinkpress.com)

Contents

Introduction

This book is for the rebels with a reason, the compliance leads who actually care, the founders who refuse to play small. It's for the quality assurance directors, heads of regulatory, compliance managers, CEOs and decision-makers working at the sharp end of regulated industries.

You operate in high-stakes markets like consumer electronics, children's toys, cannabis products, cosmetics, personal protective equipment (PPE), novel nicotine, adult toys and chemicals. Your products are innovative, your ambitions are global and your job is anything but easy.

You're not just navigating compliance, you're also juggling it across multiple countries, frameworks and risk levels. You're expanding into new markets with your name, your reputation and sometimes even your personal liability on the line.

You believe in doing things properly. You care about ethics and consumer protection. You know that 'we didn't know' won't hold up when things go wrong. You're tired of mediocrity, of firefighting, second-guessing and chasing regulators for clarity that never comes. You want structure. You want strategy. You want a way to turn compliance into something that helps you win.

This book is a framework for the ambitious, the responsible and the brave, those who know that when done right, compliance is a competitive edge not a chore. If that sounds like you, let's go.

From accidental insider to reluctant crusader

Let me be honest from the start. I didn't wake up one morning dreaming about regulatory compliance. I didn't leap out of bed thinking, 'You know what would really light my fire? A beautifully structured technical file.' Like many entrepreneurs, I reacted to an opportunity. I was exiting a shambolically run compliance company when a client looked me in the eye and said, 'Maybe it's time you started your own shop.' So I did. That client became my first customer and Arcus Compliance was born.

At the time, I didn't see myself as a crusader. Compliance was just a way to build a business and do it better than the cowboys I'd left behind. That changed. As I got deeper into the novel-nicotine industry, I saw the potential it held. Vaping wasn't just a product, it was a lifeline, a tool for harm reduction, a way to give people their breath and their lives back.

I've lost my dad and both paternal grandparents to smoking-related illnesses. That grief hardwired something in me. What began as a reactive business decision became a personal mission. Compliance stopped being a service, it became a weapon. A way to empower the good guys – the challenger brands – to stand toe to toe with Big Tobacco, to disrupt the insidious giants who've made billions selling death in shiny packaging. The early pioneers in vape weren't in it for the money, they were in it because they'd watched someone they loved die. They believed there had to be a better way and they were right. Those are the people I stand beside – the people I built Arcus for.

The landscape shifted, and the second wave came of investors and opportunists with no history, no grief, no mission, just spreadsheets and exit strategies. With them came corner cutting, non-compliance and brands built on bluster. That's when I realised compliance wasn't just about paperwork, it was about drawing a line, protecting consumers and defending the real entrepreneurs from the parasites. I started working more closely with enforcement bodies, helping them identify the bad actors. Not all of them were malicious; some were just clueless. That's the beauty of this work: when you educate the right people, you don't just remove risk, you create advocates and you raise the standard for everyone.

As Arcus grew, so did the industries we served. Clients who trusted us with vape began moving into cannabis and sexual wellness then cosmetics, toys, PPE and consumer electronics – I've now worked with some of the most disruptive and heavily regulated sectors in the world. What we found is that good compliance – built on agile systems, risk thinking and a strong culture – translates across industries. Combine that with first-class customer service and you have a winning formula. My mission has always been the same: to empower challenger brands with the tools, insight and confidence to take on the giants.

Along the way, we've created industry firsts. We delivered the UK's first formal compliance guidance for nicotine pouches. We built VIGIL, the first white-label, multilingual post-market surveillance (PMS) tool that lets brands monitor global adverse events in up to twenty-eight languages. We also helped some of the world's biggest novel nicotine, consumer electronics, cosmetics and adult toy brands navigate some of the toughest regulatory challenges out there. Not by playing it safe but by showing how compliance – done properly – can be a true growth driver, not just a legal tick-box.

Regulations overlap and lean against one another, but the foundations are the same. If you build the right frameworks and lead with customer care, technical expertise and integrity, you can win in any regulated market. What sets my company apart is our refusal to settle. We believe in proactive compliance, clear guidance and putting consumer safety at the heart of every decision.

This guidebook is the result of that work, built to help founders, brand owners and regulatory rebels like you lead with confidence, clarity and integrity.

I know what you're dealing with

Let's be honest, you're probably overwhelmed by the volume of compliance obligations you're expected to manage while trying to grow a business. Every market has its own rules, interpretations and moving goalposts. One day you're planning a launch, the next you're bogged down in documentation, labelling revisions or vague regulatory threats that leave you paralysed.

I see it all the time: the stress, the reputational risk, the uncertainty. One wrong move and it's not just your brand on the line, it's you. I've seen great products buried by regulatory confusion, while bad actors cut corners and damage entire industries.

I wrote this book because you deserve better. You deserve to know what 'good' looks like, how to get there and how to protect your business without losing your mind or your margin. I know how it feels to sit between ambition and anxiety – to want to grow but to feel like the system is built to keep you out. I don't care if you're not from a corporate background. I'm not either – I'm tattooed, plain-spoken and allergic to bullshit – but I care about truth, doing the right thing, consumer safety and giving the Davids of the world the tools to take on the Goliaths.

This book exists to help you take control, so you can turn compliance into your edge. Compliance doesn't need to be boring, it doesn't need to be just box-ticking. Done right, it's your competitive advantage.

Welcome to *The Compliance Edge*. Let's sharpen it.

The mission: Empowering bold innovators

This book isn't for the people who are comfortable, coasting or happy to blend in, play it safe and follow the same worn-out playbook the industry has been recycling for decades. This book is for the builders, the doers, those staring down at a broken system and thinking, 'There's got to be a better way.' It's for the bold innovators, the founders, creators and rebels who are tired of getting blocked, delayed, overcharged or buried under a mountain of bureaucracy built to protect the status quo.

If that's you, know this: You are exactly who I wrote this book for. I've seen what it takes for a challenger brand to rise, to punch through the noise, to take on the slow-moving giants who think their market dominance is guaranteed.

It's not just grit, though you'll need plenty of that. It's not just a killer product, although without one you're dead in the water. The thing that moves the needle – that separates the brands that scale from the brands that stall – is clarity. Clarity about what's expected of you. Clarity about the rules of the game you've chosen to play. Clarity about how to build systems and processes, and a culture that doesn't just keep you in the game but lets you win it.

Once you have that clarity, everything changes. You stop second-guessing, firefighting and living in fear of enforcement, audits or retailer rejections. You start moving with purpose, building momentum and owning your growth.

Make no mistake, the multinationals you're up against have armies behind them: legal teams, compliance departments and entire divisions whose only job is to manage risk, interpret regulations and navigate the complexity of regulated markets.

Here's what they don't have:

- You

- Your speed

- Your flexibility

- Your story

- Your face on the website, your voice on the podcast or your mission that actually means something to real people

- Your scrappy, founder-led energy

- Your ability to pivot, adapt and outmanoeuvre them while they're still scheduling their next meeting

Most importantly, they don't have your why.

When you combine that why with a set of compliance systems that are fit for purpose – agile, risk-based and built to match your ambition – you become dangerous in the best possible way. The kind of dangerous that lets you go toe to toe with anyone in the industry and win.

I want this book to give you the edge, the insight, the confidence to step into regulated markets not as the underdog but as the underestimated. Let the big players underestimate you at their peril. Let them believe you're not ready, not serious, not compliant, not scalable, then watch their faces when you prove otherwise. When your systems are clean, when your documentation is watertight, when your audits pass the first time, when your packaging gets signed off without a hitch, when the enforcement officer looks through your files and says, 'Fair play.'

That's power. That's leverage. That's how you win.

When founders like you are armed with the right strategy and the right mindset, you don't just succeed, you raise the bar. You force the industry to get better, you protect your customers and you build a business you can be proud of. That's not a side effect, that's the mission. It's the mission behind Arcus, it's the mission behind this book, it's the mission behind every conversation I have with a founder who refuses to settle for mediocrity.

This isn't about ticking boxes. It's about levelling the playing field and turning the thing most people dread – compliance – into a weapon for growth. If you're building something real, something meaningful, and you're not afraid to do things properly, you're exactly who this book was written for.

What you'll gain from this book

This isn't theory, it's a proven framework that I've used to help real brands win in complex, regulated markets. Here's what you'll take away:

- **Clarity in the chaos.** Using the ARC Scorecard, you'll assess your current compliance maturity and identify the real gaps putting your business at risk.

- **Systems that scale.** You'll build agile, fit-for-purpose compliance systems that flex with your growth and keep you ahead of change.

- **Real risk control.** With a risk-based approach, you'll identify threats early, build a live risk register and deploy mitigation strategies that work.

- **A culture that protects your brand.** Through the ARC pillars, you'll create a culture of accountability, ownership and leadership. Compliance becomes everyone's business.

- **Strategic advantage.** Core compliance gives you the six essentials to scale ethically, gain trust and turn regulation into a growth lever.

- **Peace of mind.** No more guessing, no more fire drills. You'll reduce personal exposure and protect your brand with confidence.

Most importantly, you'll stop seeing compliance as a box to tick and start using it as the strategic weapon it was meant to be.

The core compliance process: Your roadmap to strategic advantage

Most compliance advice is either outdated, defensive or built to protect large multinationals, not the disruptive founder like you. That's why I built a new model, one that helps founders lead with clarity, not fear.

Here's the process we walk through:

1. **Benchmark your compliance maturity.** We begin with the ARC Scorecard. This sharp, honest tool highlights your current position, identifies risk and sets the stage for improvement.

2. **Build agile systems that actually work.** Learn how to create adaptive compliance systems that move with your business, not against it. No templates, no fluff, just systems that get results.

3. **Own your risk before it owns you.** I'll guide you through building a live risk register and identifying key threats so you're not caught off guard. Prevention will become your superpower.

4. **Create a compliance culture that sticks.** Discover how to embed compliance into your culture so

it's not just one person's problem, it becomes part of how your business thinks and operates.

5. **Implement the six pillars of core compliance.** Finally, we lock it in with core compliance: the six universal principles every regulated business needs to scale with confidence and integrity.

This process transforms compliance from a burden into a backbone. It sets you up to scale globally, build trust and outpace competitors who are still winging it.

From confusion to clarity, from pressure to power. Let's get to work.

1
From A Shove To A Stand

My company wasn't born out of strategy; it started with a shove. I walked away from a chaotic compliance outfit with no grand plan, just a burning need to do things better. At first, compliance was just a service, a way to make a living, but it quickly became something deeper. I saw how regulation could be weaponised: sometimes to protect, sometimes to block, sometimes to punish. I'd lost people I loved to smoking-related disease, and I wasn't about to sit back while corner cutters flooded the market with unsafe products. That long-buried grief lit a fire, that fire became purpose and that purpose brought me to where I am today.

Giving the good guys teeth

Arcus was built for challenger brands, and while we started in the regulated vape sector – one of the most heavily scrutinised, fast-moving and misunderstood markets out there – we followed the pivots of our clients. As one client moved into the cannabis sector, they only wanted us to handle their compliance so we learned compliance for cannabis and hemp. As the next moved into sexual wellness, we engaged our knowledge of CE and UKCA to support them and learned cosmetics regulations along the way.

This isn't just about reading the regulations – anyone can do that and tick boxes. What actually matters – what separates success from failure – is understanding the regulations, not just reading them. It's about recognising the unique risk profile of each business, at that specific moment in their growth, and asking:

- What's the risk?

- Where's the exposure?

- What can we afford to do now?

- What should we defer?

- How do we build a compliance strategy that fits the budget, risk appetite, commercial model and growth plan, without compromising safety or integrity?

The heart of what you do should be pragmatic, strategic compliance. Compliance that becomes a sharp edge, not a blunt instrument; a weapon for growth, not a ball and chain holding you back. You need to exist to give the good guys teeth: the founders who want to scale something meaningful, protect consumers and hold the line against a flood of low-quality, non-compliant and dangerous products.

The brain surgeon vs the field medic

I'm often asked: What makes Arcus different from our competitors? I always thought it was our customer service, and it's only in recent years that I've managed to understand what it truly is: the senior management team all come from manufacturing backgrounds and truly understand the client's needs. We aren't about reading a regulation and forcing the rules on everyone to comply with; we understand the needs of start-ups, of growth and scaling companies, and we help them focus on what's important to them.

Here's the uncomfortable truth about most traditional compliance consultancies: They operate like brain surgeons. It's slow, clinical and expensive. Everything is siloed and hyper-specialised. The default approach is to tick every box, regardless of cost, practicality or relevance to your actual enforcement risk, with no consideration for budget or thought for your growth stage. This is compliance designed for multinationals with million-pound legal teams, not for founders fighting for market share while juggling supply chains, cash flow, investors and product development.

We don't work like that; instead we are the field medics. We don't prescribe brain surgery when all that is needed is a tourniquet and a clear recovery plan. We're not in an operating theatre but a battlefield, with regulators breathing down our necks, retailers demanding paperwork yesterday, customers expecting safety and competitors hoping we slip up. We come from the real world and we know what it's like to make tough decisions when time and money are tight.

Our job is triage first, and we must consider:

- What's the immediate risk?

- Where are you exposed right now?

- What must be fixed today and what can be staged over the next three, six or twelve months?

We stabilise the situation, get you compliant enough to move forward and then build long-term systems that grow with you. Everything maps back to your risk, your growth stage and your budget. This is compliance for entrepreneurs, not for bureaucrats or multinational corporations.

We're here to tip the scales and to help build a world where doing things properly is a competitive advantage, not a handicap. Where compliance isn't a burden slapped on at the last minute, but a strength baked into the business from day one. Where founder-led brands can scale globally because they've earned the right to: their products are safe, their systems are sound and their reputation is bulletproof.

We exist to arm the challengers and the disruptors. The ones who care about more than just margins, the ones who believe protecting consumers and building a real business should be the winning formula, not the shortcut merchants or the race-to-the-bottom sellers.

The non-negotiables

For successful compliance, your company needs to:

- **Tell the truth, even when it's uncomfortable.** No sugar-coating. If it's not good enough, say so to your clients, partners or regulators. That's how trust is built.
- **Simplify the complex.** Regulations are hard, so make them easier to understand, more practical and actionable so your client can focus on building their business.
- **Side with founders, not faceless corporations.** Do not prop up legacy brands or bloated conglomerates, but exist for the entrepreneurs betting everything on doing it right.

- **Obsess over consumer safety.** Whether it's a vape, a cosmetic, a sex toy or a child's toy, if it's going into someone's body, home or hands, it must be safe. No exceptions.

- **Don't chase everyone; only the right ones.** Be selective and care about long-term success, consumer trust and real compliance. Don't just look for the cheapest way to tick a box.

TRUE STORY: Agency vs in-house compliance

This one still makes me shake my head. Honestly, it still winds me up. A couple of years ago, we had a client come to us: a fast-growing brand with young, sharp founders. They were killing it on socials, viral campaigns, influencer collaborations, constant sell-outs and you could feel the momentum. True disruptors in their space.

Like a lot of brands that scale fast, they hit that 'oh sh*t' moment. That quiet internal whisper: 'Do we actually... know if we're compliant?'

Panic button pressed, they came to us. We jumped on it with a full GAP analysis of packaging, product safety, safety data sheet (SDS) authoring, labelling, PMS and retailer onboarding docs all mapped out and ready to improve. A £5K a month retainer with clear deliverables and a clear timeline. A 'plug us in and we'll handle it'-type deal.

And then? Nothing. No 'we need to think about it', no questions, just silence.

I figured something was up and checked LinkedIn a few weeks later. There it was:

'Excited to welcome our new head of compliance.'
A nice photo, balloons in the background and the obligatory caption about 'taking compliance seriously'.

They'd made a full-time hire. £80K salary, plus onboarding, pension, perks and the hidden cost no one budgets for: the six months it takes to get someone up to speed.

I've got nothing against in-house. Sometimes it's the right call, and if you've got a big product range, multiple territories and a constant stream of new launches, fair enough.

Here's the problem: Three months later, my phone rings. It wasn't a friendly check-in; it was full-blown panic. You could hear it in the voice: stressed, clipped and that edge when someone's trying to sound calm but is barely holding it together. It turned out the shiny new compliance lead wasn't quite the safe pair of hands they'd hoped for.

They:

- Didn't know the difference between a Declaration of Conformity and a technical file
- Didn't realise Safety Data Sheets needed to be authored in every language for the countries they were shipping to in the EU
- Had never logged into RAPEX
- Didn't know what PMS even looked like

The cherry on top? They approved a label that had been flagged in France. The product was pulled from the shelves and there was a national recall.

The timing couldn't have been worse. It was right before a major retail rollout they'd been chasing for months. Deadlines missed, shelf space gone, refunds issued, apologies made... all that energy building trust with retailers, wiped out in a week.

Guess who they called? We picked it up. No judgement, no 'told you so', just fix-it mode. We pulled together the technical files, reworked the SDS, updated the packaging, liaised with enforcement and brokered a resolution. We got them out of the hole, but it cost them triple what the original retainer would have been – and that's just the financial aspect. The real cost? Lost momentum, lost trust and a dent in their reputation that won't fully heal because retailers remember, enforcement bodies remember and, worst of all, the founders remember.

They knew it was avoidable.

IN-HOUSE | AGENCY

Agency vs in-house compliance: Why choosing an in-house compliance team often ends up costing more than just salary

Final word

If you're weighing up whether to bring someone in instead of getting a specialist compliance team on retainer, let me leave you with this: We don't need six weeks of onboarding, we don't need a brand book, we don't ask what RAPEX is.

We show up. Day one. Plug in. Find the risks, fix the problems, protect the brand before it becomes a headline and an expensive lesson.

It's your call. Pay for peace of mind now or pay for clean-up later. Either way, we'll be here.

2
Turning Compliance Into Competitive Advantage

For most founders, compliance feels like a burden. It's that annoying checklist in the background, the thing you know you should deal with but it never feels urgent until it is. It feels like something that slows you down, that costs you money, that gets in the way of the creative, exciting work: launching products, growing the brand and winning customers.

That's exactly why it becomes a competitive advantage. Most of your competitors feel the same. They leave it until later, treat it like an afterthought and hope they don't get caught.

Here's the uncomfortable truth. In regulated markets, compliance isn't optional and it's not a nice-to-have.

It's the price of entry, and the cost of being allowed to play the game.

Turning compliance from a burden into a business asset

How you approach compliance can make or break your business. If you treat it like a tick-box exercise, it will behave like one – a necessary evil, a dead weight, something that burns cash, slows growth and creates friction at every stage. If you flip it and treat it with the same energy, creativity and discipline that you apply to your product or your marketing, it becomes something else entirely – a moat, a ring-fence, a weapon. It becomes a reason customers trust you, retailers choose you and regulators look elsewhere.

Let's look at the big players, the household names, the blue-chip corporates. They have entire compliance departments – sometimes more than one. Teams of lawyers, quality managers, regulatory officers and risk analysts who follow the rules to the letter. They document everything, they have standard operating procedures (SOPs), internal audits, traceability systems and processes for every scenario. They often go above and beyond; partly to protect themselves and partly because that's how large, slow-moving machines operate.

Here's the twist. For all that process, they rarely connect. There's no face behind the compliance, no story, no founder explaining why the business exists, why safety matters or why trust is non-negotiable. To consumers, regulators and retailers, it all feels faceless, cold and hollow.

That is exactly where the opportunity lies for challenger brands. You're not faceless, you're visible. You're the founder on the website, the voice on the podcast, the person on the stage. You've got a story, a mission and a reason why you started. When you combine that purpose-driven founder energy with compliance systems that are lean, agile and designed around your business, you create something powerful. You're not just compliant, you're credible. You're trusted and bulletproof in ways the corporates can't copy. Here's the truth: Big companies can buy process but they can't buy authenticity. They can't fake a founder who actually cares.

When you understand compliance, when you stop outsourcing the thinking and design your systems around real risks, real products and your real growth plan, it becomes a lever for scale. It's not just a shield to block fines, it's a speed advantage, a trust signal, a marker that says: 'We take this seriously'. That's the shift.

Most brands wait, they react, they scramble when a new regulation drops. They panic when a retailer asks for a certificate they've never heard of. They cross their fingers when the shipment hits customs. Disruptive brands don't wait, they bake compliance into the business from day one. They use agile systems, risk-based decisions and a culture of ownership to move faster, not slower.

That's what the ARC methodology is built for. Not just to avoid fines, not just to stay legal but to build operational and compliance maturity. A foundation that scales, survives scrutiny and speeds up growth instead of stalling it.

When your systems are robust; when your risk register is a live radar, not a forgotten file; when your team owns compliance without hand-holding, you win. You're audit-ready, retailer-ready, investor-ready, expansion-ready.

Your competitors? They're still up at 2am fixing a label error before customs seizes the shipment. Still Googling 'What is a Declaration of Conformity?' while the enforcement officer waits in reception.

Compliance isn't just about being legal. It's not about ticking boxes. It's about resilience, confidence and durability. It's about knowing that your foundation can handle what's next:

- A new retailer? Handled.

- A new market? Covered.

- A surprise audit? Bring it.

- Investor due diligence? No problem.

The best brands don't wait for the knock on the door. They build the advantage early, quietly, intentionally. That's what this book is about.

Changing perspective and weaponising compliance for your advantage is something to consider

Seven truths of being a manufacturer in a regulated industry

If you are in the business of creating products for human use or consumption – whether that's cosmetics, novel nicotine, adult toys, PPE or anything that touches the human body – then you've entered one of the most heavily regulated arenas on the planet. It doesn't matter how innovative, exciting or disruptive your product is, the moment you enter a regulated market, you are playing by a different set of rules. This isn't the Wild West; you can't wing it and hope for the best. The reality is simple: these industries are regulated, relentless and increasingly complex. Regulations aren't loosening, they're tightening. Scrutiny isn't going away, it's growing.

Most founders don't start their journeys thinking, 'I'd love to become a compliance expert.' The moment you choose to launch products into these markets – physical or digital – you inherit that responsibility. You might not have asked for it, but it's now a core part of the game.

If you want to survive, scale and thrive in this space, there are some hard truths you need to face. These are not optional lessons; they are the foundations that separate serious brands from those that get fined, shut down or quietly disappear.

Hard truth 1: Compliance isn't optional, it's the price of entry

There's no shortcut. Compliance isn't something you can opt out of, it's not a nice-to-have or a suggestion. It's the minimum requirement to be allowed in the market.

Some founders convince themselves that if they stay small, fly under the radar or avoid certain countries, they can delay compliance. Hoping regulators won't notice is not a strategy, it's wishful thinking at best and negligence at worst.

Brands that treat compliance like an afterthought are usually the first to be pulled off the shelves. Marketplaces delist them, retailers refuse to stock them and regulators issue fines, recalls or worse.

Compliance isn't a barrier to entry, it *is* the entry.

Hard truth 2: You have a duty of care whether you like it or not

It doesn't matter what you're selling. When consumers use your product, they are trusting you – trusting that it's safe, that it won't cause harm and that you've done your homework.

If that trust is broken and someone gets hurt or becomes ill, excuses won't save you. You don't get to point fingers at your supplier, your manufacturer or the lab. The liability rests with the brand whose name is on the box.

Regulators expect that responsibility, retailers demand it and consumers assume it. Whether you like it or not, you are accountable for ensuring your product is safe, compliant and fit for purpose.

Hard truth 3: Ignorance will never be a defence

Not knowing the rules doesn't exempt you from following them. You might be unaware of what's required or you may have never read the regulations, but that won't matter when enforcement shows up. There is no grace period for not knowing. You are expected to comply, to have your documentation ready, to be aware.

When Trading Standards or EU equivalents walk through the door, they won't accept 'I didn't know' as a valid reason. Whether it's missing labelling, outdated certificates or sloppy declarations, the fault lands with you.

Hard truth 4: Growth without governance will eventually collapse

It's tempting to focus on the exciting parts of growth: new product launches, influencer campaigns, international expansion. Sales build, momentum picks up, everything feels like it's working.

If the operational side is weak – missing documentation, without risk assessments, with gaps in testing – those cracks will eventually show.

You may not feel it now, and your customers may not notice, but the pressure is building. When enforcement comes, or when your product fails or a retailer starts asking hard questions, the business can unravel fast. Small problems at the start-up stage turn into serious liabilities when you start scaling.

Hard truth 5: Non-compliance is a hidden tax on short-term thinking

Some brands cut corners. Testing looks expensive, technical files seem like admin, compliance support feels like overhead... so they skip it, they guess, they hope. It works... until it doesn't.

The money saved upfront is an illusion. When something breaks down – a failed lab test, a consumer injury or a product recall – the cost is always far greater than doing it right from the start. This is the tax on short-term thinking. It comes in lost revenue, delisting, reputational damage, legal bills, and in the worst cases, total collapse.

Smart founders know that compliance isn't a cost, it's protection. It's investment in business continuity.

Hard truth 6: Your supply chain can make or break you

Many founders put too much trust in their manufacturers. They hear 'yes, it's compliant' and assume everything's fine. This is one of the most dangerous assumptions in any regulated market.

Regulators don't audit the factory, they audit the brand. The name on the packaging is what matters.

You are the responsible person. You must hold the compliance documents, the risk assessments, the certificates. If your supplier cuts corners or hands over weak documentation, it's you who takes the fall.

Trust is not enough. You need proof. Audit them, question them and if they don't meet your standards, be prepared to walk away.

Hard truth 7: Smart brands turn compliance into a competitive advantage

The best in the industry don't treat compliance as a burden, they use it as a tool.

Strong compliance earns retailer trust. It reassures consumers and builds investor confidence. It makes your business harder to copy, harder to catch and harder to take down.

It creates a moat. When you're audit-ready, others won't be. When you're clean, others are scrambling. When you scale, others stall.

Smart brands don't avoid compliance. They lean into it and let it fuel their growth.

Final word

No founder starts a business because they love compliance, but the ones who build lasting companies are those who embrace it, master it and use it to their advantage.

The choice is simple: treat compliance as a burden and stay in survival mode, always putting out fires, or treat it as a strategy and use it to build a resilient, scalable, respected brand.

You are in the jungle now. The question is whether you survive by luck or thrive by design.

3
The ARC Mindset

ARC is a practical system for founders who take compliance seriously and want to turn it into a competitive edge. The ARC methodology is designed to highlight and identify the tools, processes and mindset shifts that will elevate and protect your brand while ensuring you remain compliant as you grow. Think of this as a framework, not a step-by-step roadmap. It's a system that challenges you to look at your business critically, dig into the details and actually do the work. This isn't something you can skim and magically emerge compliant; it requires you to roll your sleeves up, research your markets and implement what's right for your brand.

Let's be clear: this book provides the blueprint to guide you – the implementation is on you. The philosophy is simple: information is free; implementation is where the real work happens.

Regulations shift, so must you

If there's one absolute certainty in regulated markets, it's this: Nothing stays still for long. Regulations evolve, scientific opinions shift and enforcement priorities change, often without warning. What was compliant last year might be borderline this year and illegal the next. A new testing methodology might be introduced, a legal definition might change, a political decision – even if it is unrelated to your sector – can ripple through and impact your product line almost overnight.

This is not a theory. It's not something that happens to 'other' companies. It's the daily reality in fast-moving, high-stakes industries like novel nicotine, cosmetics, adult toys, PPE and consumer electronics. It affects founders and brands. It touches every decision, from product design to marketing claims.

One day, you're confident and fully compliant. The next, a regulator publishes new guidance, an enforcement body interprets something differently from others or a standards body revises a protocol and suddenly you're exposed. Your documentation is outdated, your labelling is off and your product now requires tests you weren't planning for. This isn't rare; this is normal.

Static businesses don't survive in dynamic markets. When regulation is constantly shifting, the one thing you cannot afford is rigidity. If your systems are fixed in place, if compliance is treated as a one-time project, if you're relying on what worked last year, you're building in fragility.

That approach is a time bomb. It might not go off today, it might not blow up tomorrow but it will. Whether it's triggered by a surprise audit, a delisting or a regulatory overhaul, the outcome is always the same: panic, lost revenue and reputational damage.

Founders often learn this the hard way. They assume that once the certificates are issued, the technical files are written and the labels are checked, the job is done. But compliance is not a box, it's a moving target.

Agility: An insurance policy not a buzzword

Agility means being able to absorb change without falling apart. It means adapting when the rules shift, without stalling growth, burning out your team or blowing up your operations. It's how resilient businesses stay compliant and competitive, no matter what chaos is happening around them. Agility gets tossed around in business circles, but in regulated markets it's not a cliché, it's survival.

Agility protects you from:

- New test methods that have suddenly become mandatory

- Shifting enforcement focus on claims, ingredients or packaging

- Instant policy changes by retailers or marketplaces

- Political decisions that cause almost-overnight legal changes

If your systems are agile, those changes become manageable, not existential.

Agility, the first principle of the ARC methodology, is the first principle behind building a brand that is compliant, resilient and ready for scale. Without it, you're gambling; with it, you're building something that can survive, adapt and grow, no matter how rough the landscape gets.

The two traps that kill brands

Most founders – especially those who are product-first rather than regulation-first – fall into one of two traps.

1. **Waiting for clarity.** These brands hit pause the moment something feels uncertain – they

stop launches, delay expansion, hold off on innovation and wait for someone else to give them permission to move – but clarity rarely arrives in a neat package. Regulations are often vague, open to interpretation or deliberately broad to cover different risks. Waiting for perfect clarity leads to paralysis.

2. **Blind acceleration.** These are the brands that push forward without understanding the rules. They ignore uncertainty, assume everything will be fine and hope they won't get caught. It works, until it doesn't. They grow fast then they hit a wall. A failed audit, a product recall or an enforcement action wipes out their momentum in a single blow.

Neither trap is a strategy, they're gambles. Eventually, the house wins.

The third path: The ARC mindset

Smart founders take a different route: they adopt an ARC mindset. They don't wait and they don't wing it. They stay proactive, knowing change is inevitable, and they build their business to absorb it. This isn't about moving recklessly fast; it's about moving deliberately with your eyes open, ready for the ground to shift beneath you.

The ARC mindset is built on three beliefs:

1. **Agility must be built into your operations.** Compliance systems should flex and adapt as rules evolve.

2. **Risk is only manageable when it's visible.** You need a live, accurate risk register that surfaces issues before they explode.

3. **Culture beats policy.** A team that understands its compliance role will outperform any stack of static documents.

When something changes – a new rule, a retailer request or a supply chain issue – agile brands don't panic. They plug it into their process, adapt and keep moving.

Regulation becomes a current: Once you embrace agility, something powerful shifts. Regulation stops feeling like a brick wall you keep crashing into. It starts behaving like a current; you move with it instead of fighting it. You read the signs, anticipate the direction and position yourself ahead of the wave.

When regulations tighten, you're already there. When markets open, you move faster than the competition. When enforcement sweeps hit, your house is in order.

Agility becomes a growth engine, not just a defensive shield.

The real beginning of compliance is mindset, not paperwork. The ARC methodology doesn't begin with technical files or checklists – those are outputs. It begins with mindset. A mindset that accepts the reality of regulated markets; that treats compliance as a core business function, not an annoying cost; that sees change as normal, not a crisis.

This mindset separates serious founders from the ones just getting by.

One guarantee: Regulation will keep changing. This isn't a maybe, it's a fact. Regulation will evolve, science will shift, market demands will grow, politics will interfere and your business will feel the impact.

The question isn't whether change is coming. It's whether you're built to handle it or built to break.

The ARC methodology: Turning compliance into a competitive weapon

The ARC methodology wasn't born in a boardroom. It wasn't crafted by academics or consultants chasing theory. It was built out of necessity, forged in the trenches of real businesses navigating the chaos of regulated markets. Too many founders were stuck in survival mode, using outdated systems and following vague, recycled advice. Duct-taping together internet templates, or worse, hoping no one would notice the gaps. It was a recipe for disaster. For many, that disaster came through product recalls, enforcement notices, marketplace bans or public safety scandals.

ARC was created to break that cycle. It's a framework designed specifically for founders, operators and teams who want to build credible, compliant and scalable businesses without drowning in red tape.

ARC stands for:

1. Agile systems

2. Risk-based approach

3. Compliance culture

Together, these three pillars form a living methodology that adapts to your business, shields it from risk and supports growth at every stage. This isn't a checklist or a box-ticking exercise, it's the operating framework for doing business in a regulated world.

Where do you stand?

Before diving deeper into ARC, start by asking yourself one question: Where am I right now?

Visit www.arcmethodology.com to access a free score-card tool to help you figure that out. It takes five minutes and delivers a tailored report that highlights your strengths, exposes your weak spots and gives you a roadmap to improve. Whether you're starting out or already scaling, this tool shows how closely your business aligns with the ARC methodology and where the cracks are forming.

Pillar 1: Agile systems

In regulated markets, change is constant. The rules evolve, test methods update, enforcement priorities shift, customers demand more, marketplaces tighten policies and suppliers change or fall short. If your systems can't keep up, your business will fall behind. Agile systems are built for this.

Agility is not optional, it's operational

It's not about speed for speed's sake. It's about operational flexibility – building systems that absorb change without chaos.

Agile systems are not static Word docs, dusty folders on a shared drive or PDFs buried in inboxes. They are:

- Live documents that evolve with your products, processes and regulations

- Version control that ensures teams use the latest information

- Clear workflows with assigned trackable tasks

- Integrated compliance checks tied to every launch or update

- Cloud-based systems that are easy to access and simple to update

What agility looks like in practice

You're preparing to launch a new product variant, flavour, ingredient or format. In a rigid system, panic sets in. Where are the templates? Who owns the file? Is testing complete? Are the labels right? Everything grinds to a halt.

In an agile system, it's smooth. You click 'New SKU' and a checklist populates, responsibilities are auto-assigned, templates are ready, testing is booked based on classification and packaging gets reviewed before print. No scrambling, no missing steps. Agility isn't about rushing; it's about moving without friction.

Why agile systems matter more as you grow

At start-up stage, disorganisation hides. You can get away with it when you have three stock keeping units (SKUs) and one sales channel, but when you're managing dozens of SKUs, shipping internationally and working with multiple partners, chaos compounds. Mistakes multiply and delays cost more.

Agile systems let you scale without falling apart.

Pillar 2: Risk-based approach

A common founder mistake is treating all compliance tasks the same. That leads to overwhelm. Teams obsess over low-risk details while ignoring real threats.

A risk-based approach cuts through the noise. It starts with better questions:

- Where are we exposed?
- What would be catastrophic vs inconvenient?
- What attracts regulatory attention?
- What could get us delisted or trigger backlash?

Resources are then focused where they matter most.

The core tool: A live risk register

A live risk register isn't an annual spreadsheet review, it's a dynamic system, tracking:

- Emerging regulatory shifts and interpretations
- High-risk ingredients, components, packaging or claims

- Supplier reliability and testing gaps
- Documentation issues and internal blind spots

It maps likelihood, impact and mitigation strategies, keeping risk visible and manageable.

Why a risk-based approach works

Regulators think in risk, as do retailers and investors. Smart founders should too.

If your vape product contains an unverified ingredient, that's a risk. If your adult toy lacks a material safety certification, that's a risk. If your cosmetic claims to 'treat eczema', that's a risk. You can't manage what you don't see. A risk-based approach surfaces what matters before it explodes.

Proactive beats reactive every time and waiting for enforcement isn't a strategy. Proactive companies are already fixing, improving and strengthening their systems before enforcement arrives.

Pillar 3: Compliance culture

Compliance fails when it's one person's job, or worse, when it's ignored until something breaks. To succeed, compliance must be cultural. It needs to live in every team, every role and every decision.

In a compliance culture:

- Product teams know that nothing ships without approval.

- Marketing understands claims rules and gets sign-off before going live.

- Procurement vets suppliers for documentation before placing orders.

- Customer service knows how to spot and escalate safety issues.

Compliance becomes a habit. It becomes normal. It becomes how your business operates. The outcome is credibility and resilience:

- Regulators see a cooperative, professional business.

- Retailers trust your product and processes.

- Investors recognise operational maturity.

- Consumers feel safe and supported.

The hidden superpower of culture

When compliance is embedded, it speeds everything up. You don't delay launches by chasing paperwork, you don't fight fires from missed steps, you don't panic when enforcement shows up. You move fast because everything is already built into your process. Culture creates speed without compromise.

ARC is a living system

This isn't a binder on a shelf or a one-time project. ARC is a living operating system. It grows with your business, prepares you for the next wave of regulation, keeps you resilient when the pressure comes and keeps you credible under scrutiny. Most importantly, it lets you focus on growth because the foundation is solid.

Final word

The ARC methodology was designed for founders. It's practical, it's flexible, it works.

Start by visiting www.arcmethodology.com and taking the free scorecard. It only takes five minutes, but the insights will last much longer.

Use it to see where you stand then use this book to start building, because compliance isn't a burden, it's your competitive edge.

4
The ARC
Methodology Venn

The ARC methodology only works when all three pillars – agile systems, risk-based approach and compliance culture – are present and integrated. Like a three-legged stool, remove one leg and the whole structure starts to wobble, tilt or collapse.

This is the daily operational reality for any founder working in regulated markets. When compliance feels like chaos, confusion, burnout or constant firefighting, it's almost always because one of the pillars is missing or underdeveloped.

The ARC methodology Venn diagram shows the relationship between agile systems, risk-based approach and compliance culture. The overlap is where businesses thrive. The gaps are where they bleed time, money and trust.

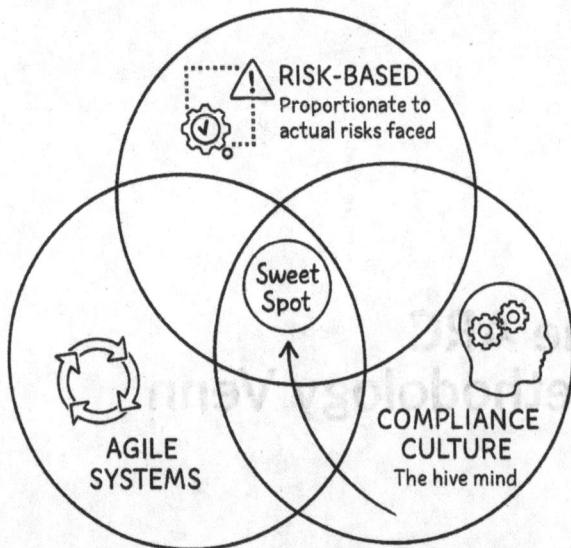

The ARC Mindset: Understanding the three pillars
of the ARC methodology and how they only work
when all three are active together

What happens when one pillar is missing?

We will now explore what happens when a missing pillar causes the ARC methodology to fail.

1. Risk-based approach + compliance culture, but no agile systems

You're doing a lot right. Your team understands the importance of compliance, you're not ignoring the risks and you have clarity on where the biggest exposures are, but the machinery is broken.

The problem: You know what needs doing but you can't move fast enough

Your processes are clunky and slow. Documents are scattered across shared drives, email threads and outdated folders. Every update feels like starting over. When a retailer asks for a technical file, it's a mad scramble. When regulations change, nobody knows who is updating what.

This creates 'scale friction'. You're stuck in reactive mode, always behind. Launches are delayed, packaging changes trigger weeks of confusion, audits are stressful, retailer questions feel like fire drills. The team knows what to do but without agility they can't execute at the pace the market demands.

Warning signs

- Endless confusion over which document version is correct

- Tasks falling through the cracks due to unclear workflows

- Growth stalls because the back end can't keep up

- Burnout rises as staying compliant starts to feel exhausting

This is where founders say

- 'We know what's required, but getting it done is exhausting.'
- 'It feels like we're always playing catch-up.'

2. Agile systems + compliance culture, but no risk-based approach

This setup looks solid from the outside. You've got systems, you've got workflows, your team takes compliance seriously, tasks get ticked off and documents are in order. Under the surface, there's a critical flaw: you're not focusing on the right risks.

The problem: You're busy, but not safe

- Without a risk-based approach, everything gets treated as equally important or decisions are based on guesswork.
- Your team spends time perfecting low-risk tasks while missing high-impact hazards.

This is operational theatre: everyone looks busy but the blind spots are massive.

Examples

- Gold-standard documentation for minor packaging tweaks, while high-risk products have expired test reports

- Detailed claims reviews for low-priority SKUs, while a major market update goes unnoticed

The team feels confident because the wheels are turning but the iceberg is dead ahead.

Warning signs

- Surprise enforcement actions for issues nobody flagged

- Wasted money on unnecessary tests

- Constant frustration: 'We're doing everything, but it still isn't enough.'

- Founders blindsided by risks they assumed were covered

This is what you hear

- 'We thought we were covered until that letter arrived.'

- 'I can't believe this slipped through after everything we've spent on compliance.'

3. Agile systems + risk-based approach, but no compliance culture

This is a technically capable business. You've got tools, you've mapped the risks and your processes are well designed, but the people aren't engaged.

The problem: The systems exist but nobody owns them

Compliance is siloed – it lives in one inbox or department. The rest of the business doesn't see it as their job. Nobody feels accountable as everyone assumes someone else is handling it.

This is the most dangerous failure point. Everything looks fine, until it doesn't.

Common failures

- A marketing campaign launches with illegal claims because no one followed the checklist.

- A product ships with outdated labels because procurement didn't raise the flag.

- A supplier changes materials and nobody notices because sign-off was skipped.

Everything seems under control until something breaks.

Warning signs

- Processes exist but are routinely ignored.

- Compliance checks are seen as annoying, not essential.

- The team blames each other when things go wrong.

- Founders discover the system was never being followed in the first place.

This is what you hear

- 'I thought the team was doing this.'

- 'We have a process but no one's following it.'

- 'How did this slip through when we had it mapped out?'

The compliance sweet spot

When agile systems, risk-based approach and compliance culture are fully active and integrated, your business enters the compliance sweet spot. This is where compliance stops being a burden and becomes a business asset:

- Documents stay current because systems are agile.

- Resources go to what matters most because risk drives priorities.

- Tasks don't fall through the cracks because everyone owns compliance.

At this point, things get easier. You move faster, you stop firefighting, retailers trust you, regulators respect you and investors see structure instead of chaos.

Most importantly, compliance becomes your engine for growth. You expand with confidence, protect your brand and sleep better at night knowing the foundation is solid.

Final word

If compliance feels painful right now – if launches are delayed, if your team is firefighting, if you're struggling to answer simple questions from regulators or retailers – then one or more of these pillars isn't fully in place. That's not failure, that's your diagnosis, and diagnosis is where the fix begins.

Coming up, we dive into compliance maturity. How each of the three pillars evolves over time, how to move from reactive chaos to resilient growth and how the ARC methodology becomes the backbone of a brand built to survive, scale and lead.

5
Agile Systems

Agile systems are neither a luxury nor nice-to-haves. In regulated industries, they are the difference between a brand that scales with confidence and one that drowns in chaos the moment anything changes.

This is not about speed for speed's sake. It's about working smarter and structuring your operations in a way that allows your business to stay compliant without suffocating under its own weight. Crucially, agile systems are not abstract. They are practical, tangible and woven into the daily rhythm of how your team operates.

The operational reality of non-agile systems

Let's start with the blunt truth. Here is what can happen if you run a business without agile systems:

- A retailer asks for a technical file and no one knows who has the latest version.

- A supply chain swap happens but nobody flags the need for updated safety assessments.

- Packaging errors are discovered after products are put on the shelf.

- Regulatory changes go unnoticed until a product is pulled from the marketplace.

- A new SKU launch turns into chaos with missed files, confused teams and last-minute fixes.

This is more than inefficiency, it is dangerous. In regulated markets, these gaps can lead to enforcement actions, lost revenue, delistings and long-term brand damage.

If any of this sounds familiar, you are not alone. This is the default state for most growing brands before agile systems are introduced.

REGULATIONS SHIFT:
SO MUST YOU

*Always consider the importance of remaining agile
and employing systems to help you adapt*

What an agile compliance system really does

An agile compliance system is not just software, a checklist or a one-off audit. It is an operating framework that holds the business together when things change.

When regulations shift, the system adapts. When a product evolves, the system keeps pace. When a new market opens, the system already knows what's needed to enter it. This is not magic; it is intentional design.

The founder's test: Is your system agile?

Ask yourself:

- If a retailer or regulator requested documentation today, how long would it take you to respond?

- When packaging is updated, who checks that the legal elements are still accurate?

- How are material changes from suppliers communicated and reviewed?

- How do you stay informed about regulatory changes in countries where you sell?

- Who owns your risk register, and how often is it updated?

If your answers start with 'it depends', your system likely needs work.

Anatomy of an agile system: The execution blueprint

Here is how high-performing regulated brands build agile systems.

1. A single source of truth for documentation

- All compliance documents are stored in a central, structured location.

- Version control is active with clear logs of what changed, when and by whom.

- Access is permission-based so the right people can edit or view, as needed.

- Obsolete documents are archived, not deleted, preserving the audit trail.

Practical outcome: No more guessing which version is current. If an inspector asks, you're ready in minutes, not days.

2. Embedded change control, not manual panic

- Any change – packaging, formulation, supplier or regulatory – triggers a workflow.

- Stakeholders across procurement, technical, marketing and compliance review each change.

- Compliance impact is assessed before anything goes live.

Practical outcome: No more products hitting shelves with non-compliant labels or unverified materials.

3. Regulatory intelligence built into the workflow

- Automated feeds and alerts track law and guidance changes in each active market.

- Updates go to the right people, not just to the founder's inbox.

- New requirements generate review tasks within the workflow.

Practical outcome: No more being blindsided. You adapt early, before regulators or retailers force your hand.

4. Packaging review as a mandatory gate, not an afterthought

- Every design file goes through a compliance checklist before print approval.

- Language, safety symbols, claims and legal formatting are validated.

- Sign-off logs confirm who reviewed what and when.

Practical outcome: No more customs delays, retail rejections or platform takedowns over label mistakes.

5. Product lifecycle compliance: From idea to post-market

- Compliance checklists are embedded from day one of product development.

- Technical files evolve as products evolve.

- PMS actively captures feedback, incidents and complaints.

Practical outcome: You are never caught off guard by safety issues or late-stage compliance failures.

6. Cross-departmental ownership

- SOPs are built to include all functions: compliance, marketing, procurement, logistics and customer service.

- Every team knows their role in keeping products compliant.

- Tasks are assigned to individuals, not departments, with clear accountability.

Practical outcome: Nothing falls through the cracks. Everyone owns compliance, not just the 'compliance team'.

7. Built-in feedback loops that learn and adapt

- Every complaint, audit or failure feeds back into process improvement.

- SOPs and workflows are reviewed regularly, not just once a year.

- Lessons learned are turned into system upgrades.

Practical outcome: The system gets smarter over time. Mistakes are fixed, not repeated.

What do agile systems feel like?

Agile systems transform the internal feel of your business. You stop firefighting, you start planning ahead. Compliance stops being friction and starts feeling like flow. Product launches become smoother, updates are faster and audits feel routine rather than catastrophic. Teams stop treating compliance as a chore; it becomes a natural part of how things work, just like sales or product development.

The hidden return on investment of agile systems

Founders often ask: 'What is the return on investing in systems like this?' The answers are:

- Faster time to market

- Fewer product delays or takedowns

- Lower enforcement risk
- Higher retailer and investor confidence
- Fewer sleepless nights

This is not cost, it's insurance, operational confidence and the freedom to grow without the fear of collapse.

Final word

Agility is not a buzzword. It is the baseline for surviving and scaling in regulated markets.

If you do not design for agility now, the cost will come later. Maybe in audits, maybe in enforcement, maybe in burnout – probably in all three.

Agility is not about speed, it is about never getting stuck.

6
Risk-Based Approach

A risk-based approach is not optional in regulated industries. It is not a bonus strategy but the foundation of staying in business.

This is not about being paranoid, it is about being precise. It is about knowing which failures are minor headaches and which are brand-ending disasters. Without it, founders fall into one of two traps:

1. Obsessing over the wrong things while real threats grow unnoticed

2. Ignoring everything and hoping luck holds out

Both paths lead to the same place: fines, product withdrawals, regulatory scrutiny, lost shelf space and reputational damage that no PR firm can fix.

Why risk-based thinking changes everything

Here is the brutal truth nobody tells founders upfront: Regulators and retailers expect you to be risk-based, marketplace compliance teams assume it and investors demand it. If your internal systems cannot show how you identify, assess, prioritise and control compliance risks then you are not a business, you are a liability.

It's important that you don't skip this. Here is what a non-risk-based business can look like:

- You are paying for lab tests on your entire portfolio yet you've never screened a single ingredient.

- Your team perfects packaging documents while ignoring PMS.

- A supplier quietly swaps out a material and nobody catches it until the regulator arrives.

- You get hit with enforcement for a label violation in a country you'd forgotten had different rules.

This is not bad luck, it is what happens when compliance is driven by guesswork instead of risk.

The risk-based playbook

Ask yourself: Can you name your top five compliance risks? Do you know which SKUs, ingredients or suppliers carry the highest exposure? If a regulator asked, could you prove how you control those risks? Do your team leads know what 'high risk' means for their function? If the answers are no, the following eight-step risk-based approach is important for you.

1. Identify risks: Find the landmines before you step on them

The most dangerous risks are the ones you never saw coming.

Start with brutal honesty and ask yourself: Where could things go wrong? What would happen if they did go wrong? How would you know? Who would be affected: the customer, retailer or regulator?

You will need to cover the following:

- **Product risks.** Ingredients, testing gaps and labelling.

- **Supply chain risks.** Missing certificates and falsified declarations.

- **Documentation risks.** Expired reports and outdated files.

- **Operational risks.** Unclear ownership and miscommunication.

- **Market risks.** Exporting without full understanding of local rules.

2. Build and maintain a living risk register

This is not an annual formality, it is a live, working tool that must be updated whenever something changes. Everyone involved should be able to access it. Risk reviews should happen monthly or quarterly, not annually.

Your risk register should include:

- **Description.** What is the risk?

- **Source.** Where does it originate?

- **Likelihood.** How probable is it?

- **Impact.** What if it does happen?

- **Owner.** Who is accountable?

- **Mitigation.** What are you doing about it?

- **Actions.** What happens next?

- **Status.** Open, in progress, mitigated or closed.

3. Score and prioritise ruthlessly

Not every risk is urgent, some are just noise. To stop wasting time on the wrong things, you need a triage system in place, using a simple formula:

Likelihood × severity = priority

For example:

- High likelihood + high severity = act immediately.

- Low likelihood + high severity = prepare mitigation in case it happens.

- High likelihood + low severity = monitor and manage.

- Low likelihood + low severity = track occasionally.

4. Mitigate: Move from risk to control

Once ranked, each risk needs mitigation. Ask yourself: How do we reduce the chance of this happening? How do we reduce the damage if it does happen?

Tactics include:

- Updating certificates or files
- Replacing suppliers

- Adding third-party testing
- Strengthening SOPs
- Training staff
- Improving escalation protocols

Every open risk must have an owner. If nobody owns it, it will be ignored until it becomes a crisis.

5. Monitor: Risk is never static

What is low risk today could become high risk tomorrow. For example, a supplier changes materials without informing you; a new regulation is passed; a competitor gets fined, putting your entire category under review; or sales expand into a new region you have not assessed.

Monitoring includes:

- Regular risk register reviews
- Feeding in complaint data and surveillance results
- Updating risks when anything changes upstream or downstream

6. Embed risk into every decision

Risk is not something compliance handles alone, it must influence:

- **Product development.** Are we adding complexity or exposure?

- **Procurement.** Can this supplier prove compliance?

- **Marketing.** Are we making risky claims?

- **Ops.** Do we know which markets require new symbols or warnings?

This is how you stop stepping on landmines.

7. Be aware of cross-functional risk

Compliance is a team sport and everyone must play their part.

- Product teams know which ingredients or materials pose risk.

- Procurement checks certifications before placing orders.

- Customer service flags complaints that hint at safety issues.

- Marketing verifies all claims align with the regs.

- Quality control catches inconsistencies before they ship.

If one function is blind, the whole business is exposed.

8. Learn fast from failure

Every failure, near miss or complaint is fuel. You must:

- Update the risk register
- Adjust SOPs
- Review your mitigations
- Share lessons internally

Smart businesses build learning into the loop; weak businesses repeat the same mistakes.

Final word

When a risk-based approach works, you stop guessing and wasting time and money on the wrong tasks. You wake up to a regulatory shift and realise the mitigation is already underway. Regulators see professionalism, retailers see trustworthiness and investors see resilience.

This is not about fear, this is about control. Risk-based thinking turns compliance from a minefield into a map. It helps founders sleep at night, not because nothing can go wrong but because they know what can go wrong and have built systems to handle it.

Risk is real, risk is manageable, and when done right, risk becomes your edge.

7
Compliance Culture

You can have the best systems, a bulletproof risk register, perfect documentation, clever software and airtight processes, but none of it matters if the culture is broken.

Compliance culture is not a policy or a poster or a paragraph in the staff handbook, it is what people do when nobody is watching. It is how they act under pressure. It is how they make decisions in the thousands of unseen moments that never appear in an audit report.

Culture is the difference between scaling safely or crashing publicly.

What a broken culture looks like

In a broken culture, the following may happen:

- A product goes live with incorrect labels because 'it was not my job to check'.

- Customer service ignores a safety complaint because 'that's compliance's problem'.

- Marketing pushes a risky claim live because 'we could not delay the launch'.

- Procurement signs off on dodgy paperwork because 'we assumed someone else reviewed it'.

The systems were there, the SOPs existed but the culture was not. This is how good companies end up with recalls, fines and front-page failures.

Why founders set the tone

If you are the founder, CEO or operator, you are the culture. If you treat compliance as a nuisance, your team will follow. If you roll your eyes at regulations, joke about 'gaming the system', or only bring up compliance when something breaks, corners get cut, checks get skipped and problems get buried.

Culture is not what you say, it is what your team feels allowed to do.

The anatomy of a strong compliance culture

As a founders culture test, honestly ask yourself:

- Does every department understand how compliance affects their role?

- Can people raise concerns, even when it delays a launch or pushes back on a senior exec?

- When things go wrong, do we look at systems or just blame individuals?

- Do we celebrate compliance wins with the same energy as revenue milestones?

- Am I modelling the behaviour I want from the team?

If the answer to any of these is no, then culture is where the work begins with the following seven stages.

1. Leadership buy-in

Culture starts at the top – always. Founders and execs cannot delegate this, they must own it.

Compliance shows up in leadership meetings as part of operations, not just emergencies. It is viewed as a growth enabler, not just a cost. If leaders value it, the team will follow. If they ignore it, so will everyone else.

2. Clear ownership

Everyone must know their piece of the puzzle. Compliance ownership is not assumed, it is documented. It lives in job descriptions, SOPs, checklists and workflows.

No more 'I thought someone else was on it'. No more grey areas. When things go wrong, the first question is not: 'Who failed?' It is: 'Where was the handover unclear?'

Clarity kills confusion. Clarity reduces risk.

3. Embedded, role-specific training

Training should not be a tick-box PowerPoint, it should be ongoing, practical and tailored to each function

- Marketing learns claim laws.

- Procurement learns how to review supplier declarations.

- Product teams understand materials and testing.

- Training gets refreshed when laws or products change or risks increase.

Use real-world case studies from your industry. Nothing grabs attention like: 'This happened to a business like ours'.

4. Speak-up culture

If your team is afraid to raise concerns, compliance fails silently.

- Does someone see a label error? Raise it before print.

- Does a supplier feel off? Flag it before the shipment arrives.

- Does a claim feel risky? Bring it up before it goes live.

No fear, no blame, no shame. Just a shared mindset that prevention beats clean-up. Leaders reinforce this by rewarding those who speak up, not punishing them for creating 'friction'.

5. Cross-functional accountability

Compliance is not a department; it is an ecosystem.

- Manufacturing owns product risks.

- Marketing owns claim risks.

- Procurement owns supplier risks.

- Customer service owns feedback risks.

One weak link exposes everyone, but when every team takes ownership, compliance becomes seamless.

6. Recognition and reinforcement

Celebrate what you want more of.

- Someone catches an error before it hits the shelves? Celebrate it.

- A team navigates a regulatory update with no disruption? Shout it out.

- Compliance passes a retailer audit? Put it in the company update.

This is not fluff, this is operational reinforcement. You get what you reward.

7. Continuous learning

Culture is not static, neither is compliance. When something breaks, use it:

- What happened?

- Where did ownership fail?

- Where did the system allow this through?

- What changes so this never happens again?

Every incident, mistake or warning letter is a chance to level up.

The hive mind

When people think of compliance, they picture paperwork, policies and ticking boxes. The truth is compliance is a living, breathing process. One of the biggest advantages compliance consultancies offer clients isn't just documentation or advice, it's what we call the 'hive mind': when one client's pain becomes everyone else's advantage.

The hive mind: By proactively reusing one client's pain to become everyone else's advantage, we create the 'hive mind'

TRUE STORY: When one client's friction becomes ten clients' foresight

Years ago, one of our vape clients came to us with something bold. They wanted to launch a new 2+10 device, something untested in the UK or EU regulatory space. Innovative, disruptive and completely uncharted.

We rolled up our sleeves, worked directly with the MHRA and several EU authorities, challenged interpretations, presented data and built arguments. It was messy, complex and high-stakes, but we got there.

The result? We helped bring the first legally compliant 2+10 innovation product to market.

Most compliance firms would stop there. They would chalk it up as a win, send the invoice and move on, but that's not how we work at Arcus. We took everything we learned – the objections, the loopholes, the evidence that changed minds – and built it into our internal playbook, then we picked up the phone.

Ten other clients had similar ambitions. Some didn't even realise their ideas would trigger the same regulatory red flags. Because of that first case, we were already ten steps ahead and they launched with clarity, without delays or fire drills, without reinventing the wheel.

That's the power of the hive mind. One client's friction becomes ten clients' foresight. When you're working alone, you only see the problems that land on your desk, but when you're part of a network, you're learning from a much wider field across sectors such as novel nicotine, consumer electronics, cosmetics, toys, cannabis, PPE and more. You get to see what's coming before most brands do because someone, somewhere in the ecosystem, has already hit the wall, and the fix is already being built.

This is not box-ticking or reactive compliance, this is collective intelligence, shared defence and proactive advantage. The hive mind means clients don't just meet the minimum standard, they stay ahead of enforcement, innovation and risk. Working with companies like Arcus doesn't just protect your brand, it gives you access to a compliance advantage that most companies never realise exists.

Final word

In compliance culture:

- Everyone knows the rules and why they exist.

- Issues are raised early, not buried.

- Risk is managed proactively, not reactively.

- Mistakes are rare and caught in planning, not post-launch.

- The team acts with care, pride and accountability.

It stops feeling like a chore and becomes 'just how we do things here'. When culture is strong: you move faster, you grow without chaos, you sleep better at night and your team works with pride.

Culture failure is the most expensive mistake a growing brand can make. If you skip compliance culture, processes get ignored, systems fall apart and risk registers gather dust. Compliance becomes a one-person job and when that person leaves, everything burns down.

Systems do not run themselves, processes do not check themselves and files do not update themselves – people do. Culture is the glue that holds your compliance infrastructure together. It is what makes systems useful and risk registers meaningful.

Documents show compliance; culture proves it.

8
The Compliance Maturity Arc

Operating in a regulated market isn't just about launching great products, it's also about navigating a complex set of rules, expectations and risks that shift as your brand grows. Compliance maturity isn't a bonus, it's a survival skill.

Every founder is somewhere on this journey, whether they realise it or not. It's an arc, a transition from naive hustle to operational resilience, and as your business scales, the rules change. Visibility brings opportunity but also attracts scrutiny.

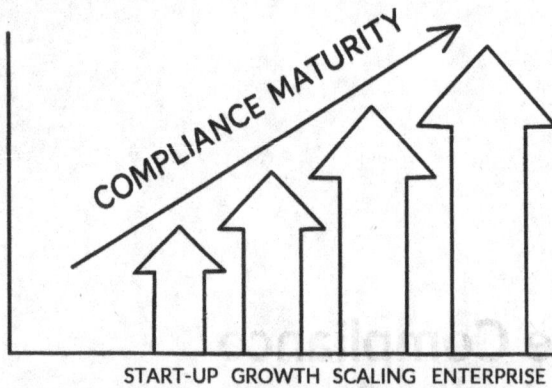

Every growing brand takes the same predictable path, where growth and compliance pressure collide to build a compliance maturity

In the earliest days, you're operating under the radar. You might be testing the waters, relying on third-party platforms or shipping small batches with minimal oversight. It feels nimble and fast but that invisibility is temporary. As revenue grows and the brand expands into new markets, everything changes. What were once minor oversights become serious liabilities. Regulators who never noticed you suddenly start paying attention.

In regulated markets, growth and enforcement risk are directly connected. If your systems and documentation don't mature with the business, you're exposed. The consequences range from fines and product recalls to marketplace bans or reputational damage that can kill momentum.

Compliance maturity is the antidote. It shifts you from reactive chaos to proactive control, preparedness not perfection. When regulators, retailers or platforms come knocking, your ability to respond confidently becomes your defence.

The four stages of the compliance maturity arc

The compliance maturity arc has four stages, as follows.

1. Start-up: Wing it and hope for the best

This is where most founders start their journey: fast, scrappy and focused on survival. There are no structured systems in place, no formal documentation to speak of. Compliance lives in the founder's head, pieced together from supplier assurances, vague industry chatter or late-night Google searches. At this stage, there's little understanding of what the regulations actually require because no one's asked the hard questions yet. It feels liberating, almost rebellious, moving fast and breaking things while bigger competitors lumber under their own weight.

This freedom comes at a cost. Founders often carry personal liability without even realising it. Their signature is on import documents, their name is tied to product registrations, and if something goes wrong, they're the first in the firing line. Enforcement risk feels low, but that's deceptive. In reality, all it takes is a single customer complaint, a curious Trading Standards officer or a random spot check to pull the curtain back. Suddenly, what felt like a minor oversight, an untested component or an outdated safety certificate, can turn into fines, recalls or even a full market ban. The danger is hidden... until it explodes into full view.

2. Growth: Welcome to the spotlight

At this stage, the brand is no longer flying under the radar. Traction is building, sales are climbing, and with that comes a new level of attention. Retailers, distributors and online marketplaces start asking the tough questions: 'Where's your technical file?' 'Can you provide safety certifications?' 'Do you have the declarations for every SKU?' For many founders, this is the first time compliance feels real, and the cracks in their systems begin to show.

Some documentation might exist, but it's often a fragile patchwork of templates hastily downloaded from the internet, supplier certificates accepted at face value without verification and files saved in random folders with no version control. It worked before because no one was checking too closely. Now, with larger orders and expanded distribution, the margin for error is gone.

Compliance remains reactive, firefighting rather than future-proofing. Issues get patched only when someone demands it, creating a false sense of progress. But as product lines grow and cross borders, complexity multiplies at speed. Each market brings its own quirks and requirements, and keeping up feels like trying to plug holes in a sinking boat.

This is where most brands encounter their first major scare: a flagged listing on Amazon that freezes cash flow overnight; a retailer issuing a take-it-or-leave-it ultimatum: 'Fix this or lose the shelf space'; a sternly worded regulatory warning that sends shockwaves through the team. Suddenly, the old way of working – gut instinct and last-minute fixes – just isn't enough. The founder realises they've stepped into the spotlight, and with visibility comes scrutiny.

3. Scale-up: Systems catch up

By now, the founder has had their wake-up call. The scares of the growth stage, the near-misses, the retailer ultimatums and the regulatory slaps on the wrist have made one thing crystal clear: guesswork doesn't scale. Survival requires structure. This is the moment they shift gears and start building compliance into the foundations of the business, rather than bolting it on as an afterthought.

Dedicated compliance support enters the picture, whether through hiring internal specialists, engaging external consultants or leaning on helpdesk models to fill the gaps. For the first time, there's a sense of ownership over compliance, not just from the founder but across the team. Processes are mapped out and documented. SOPs are created and actually followed. Critical files are version-controlled and tracked rather than buried in someone's inbox. Risks aren't just vaguely acknowledged, they're actively identified, prioritised and mitigated.

This is often where the ARC methodology starts making its mark. Agile systems replace chaotic spreadsheets. A risk-based mindset begins to guide decisions on product launches and market expansions. A compliance-led culture starts to take hold, where teams understand that regulatory readiness isn't optional, it's a competitive necessity.

Compliance becomes embedded in the company's DNA: built into development cycles, baked into packaging reviews and considered at every stage of go-to-market planning. Enforcement risk hasn't disappeared – it never will – but it's no longer an existential threat. The difference is foresight. The business is no longer reacting in a panic; it's operating with confidence and control, ready to handle challenges before they escalate.

4. Enterprise: Compliance as an asset

At this stage, compliance is no longer seen as an operational burden, it's a strategic weapon. The business has matured into an organisation where regulatory excellence isn't just expected; it's a defining part of the brand's reputation. Compliance becomes a competitive advantage, setting the company apart from rivals who are still stuck in reactive mode.

Dedicated compliance officers oversee live risk registers and real-time monitoring systems that track obligations across multiple jurisdictions. The business no longer waits for regulators to come knocking, it engages them directly, providing feedback on proposed changes and staying ahead of new legislation. This proactive approach not only reduces risk but positions the company as a trusted voice in the industry.

Documentation is audit-ready at all times. Every technical file, declaration and certificate is maintained with military precision, accessible at a moment's notice. PMS isn't a box-ticking exercise, it's integrated into customer feedback loops, allowing the company to spot trends, address issues early and feed insights back into product development.

The results are transformative. Enforcement risk doesn't vanish entirely, but it drops dramatically. Regulators respect the brand and view it as a safe operator.

Retailers see consistency and reliability, making the business their preferred partner. Investors are reassured by the robust infrastructure, seeing compliance as a sign of long-term sustainability. Consumers feel protected and that trust translates into loyalty.

At this level, compliance is no longer a cost centre, it's an enabler of growth. It protects what the founder has built, strengthens relationships with every stakeholder group and creates a platform for the business to expand into new markets with confidence. This is the destination every ambitious brand in a regulated market should aspire to.

What compliance maturity really means

Compliance maturity isn't about drowning your team in paperwork or building bloated departments full of box tickers. It's about identifying where you are on your growth journey and creating a business that's resilient, agile and trusted, because it's built on a foundation that can stand up to scrutiny.

At its core, compliance maturity means:

- **Clarity.** Knowing exactly what each market expects before you step in. No grey areas, no guesswork.

- **Ownership.** Clear responsibilities across teams and partners so nothing falls through the cracks.

- **Scalability.** Systems that grow with your business instead of collapsing under pressure during expansion.

- **Resilience.** Reduced dependency on key individuals or outdated knowledge locked in someone's head.

- **Culture.** A mindset where compliance isn't a last-minute scramble or a panic button, it's a daily habit baked into how your company operates.

When regulators, retailers or partners come asking tough questions, you're not buying time, drafting excuses or scrambling to pull together half-finished documents. Your answers are ready. Not in draft, not in progress but ready.

That's what separates the brands that survive scaling from the ones that stall or implode.

How maturity impacts enforcement risk

Enforcement isn't random. Regulators don't spin a wheel or pull names out of a hat. They're strategic. They focus their limited resources where the risks and headlines are highest.

Here's what puts a brand squarely in their sights:

- **Explosive growth and rising visibility.** The bigger your footprint, the more attention you attract.

- **Cross-border operations.** Selling into multiple markets multiplies complexity and scrutiny.

- **Negative customer feedback or complaints.** Every issue logged with a regulator is a potential trigger.

- **Poor organisation.** Brands that look unprepared signal vulnerability and invite closer inspection.

If your compliance systems are still stuck at the start-up level while your revenue and reputation are scaling, you're playing with fire. The enforcement risk isn't theoretical, it's inevitable.

Mature brands? They're not bulletproof but they're built to withstand pressure. They don't scramble when a regulator asks for documentation, they hand it over with confidence. They don't stall when laws change, they've already adjusted their processes. When problems arise, they respond swiftly, adapt and improve.

That kind of resilience does more than protect you, it builds a reputation regulators respect, retailers rely on and consumers trust. Enforcement becomes less likely; if it does happen, the damage is contained and the business keeps moving forward.

TRUE STORY: The £600,000 flavouring mistake

Let me tell you a story – a painful one that still makes my stomach turn because I watched it happen in real time, and it didn't need to.

This wasn't a cowboy outfit or a bedroom brand, it was a serious company. A good team with solid funding, an established customer base, a product roadmap, a marketing team, investor confidence – the works. They were riding high and planning their next big launch: new flavours, new packaging, new positioning. It was meant to be the brand's big step-up, their statement to the industry and, on the surface, everything looked great.

They had lined up distribution, they had marketing materials printed and ready, they had stock filled and packed, ready to ship, but there was one problem – a small one, technically. One line in a spreadsheet, one compound in a bottle, one decision made months earlier in the rush of development: they'd used a flavouring that wasn't permitted under UK regulations.

It wasn't flagged or challenged. No one asked the supplier for the compliance data or cross-checked the Chemical Abstracts Service (CAS) number. There was no toxicological review, no basic due diligence.

By the time enforcement got involved, it was too late. Retailers had already received stock, advertising was live and units had been sold to consumers.

When the alert came through, everything went into panic mode. They tried to recall, to rework the labels, to find a defence, but there wasn't one. This wasn't a technicality, it was a breach of the law.

The consequences were brutal: stock had to be destroyed, retail listings were pulled, contracts were cancelled and confidence in the brand evaporated. The final bill? Over £600,000. Gone. Not on growth or investment, just lost. Written off. Dead money.

How not screening your formulations/recipes can have a massively negative effect on your business

The founders were devastated. Not just because of the financial hit but because of what it said about their credibility. They thought they'd done everything right but the truth is, they'd skipped the most important step, the one thing that could have protected them: a full technical compliance check of their ingredients before launch.

I don't tell this story to scare you, I tell it because it's not unique. This is what happens when compliance is treated as a tick-box exercise or left to chance. It's what happens when you assume your manufacturer is taking care of it or when you think, 'That flavour's been used before, so it must be fine.' It's a mistake that I see far too often, across cosmetics, vapes, toys, electronics – you name it.

The bottom line is this: If you're operating in a regulated industry, you need to know exactly what's in your product. You need the paperwork, the toxicology/ bill of materials, the evidence that it's compliant in every market you plan to sell in because regulators are not messing about. They don't care how nice your branding is, they care about consumer safety and if you can't demonstrate that your product is safe and legal, you will lose. Quickly.

Compliance companies such as Arcus make it their mission to stop stories like this from happening by building the systems, checking the documents and catching the problems before they cost you everything.

This isn't about bureaucracy, it's about protecting your brand, your investment and your customers. Let this be your wake-up call and don't let one flavour cost you a fortune.

Final word

The world doesn't stand still. Markets evolve, consumer expectations shift and regulators rewrite the rules faster than most brands can keep up. Compliance maturity isn't a box you tick once and forget, it's a living, breathing part of your infrastructure that needs to grow and adapt with your business.

The compliance maturity arc gives you a clear framework. It shows you where you are today, where you're exposed and what you need to strengthen to survive the next stage of growth because the moment your brand starts to scale, the spotlight finds you. Someone – whether it's a regulator, a retailer or a competitor – is watching, and what happens next isn't down to luck. It's down to how ready you are.

9

The Enforcement Risk Radar

Enforcement doesn't happen by accident. It's not random, unlucky or even strictly about whether your product is technically compliant. It happens because you showed up on the radar. That radar is always on, always scanning and watching. Hunting for easy wins, big headlines and brands that make regulators look effective.

In regulated industries, enforcement isn't a distant possibility. It's not a bolt of lightning that strikes out of nowhere. It's a live, moving variable that shifts constantly based on how and where you operate and how loud you are while doing it. You may think you're flying under the radar now, but the second you start scaling, launching in new markets, hiring a sales team and pouring money into marketing, you're sending out a signal flare.

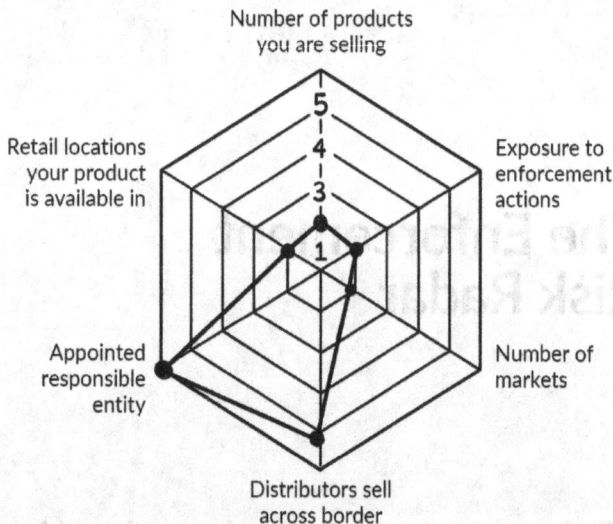

Enforcement Risk Radar: A radar map and proprietary framework for identifying a brand's likelihood of enforcement

The question isn't 'Will they notice me?' It's 'When they notice me, will I be ready?'

The Enforcement Risk Radar

Here's a truth most founders don't understand until it's too late: Regulators are not trying to audit every business equally – they don't have the resources; they don't even pretend to try. There is no universal, consistent or fair application of enforcement across the UK or EU member states. Regulators are under pressure and under-resourced, which means they are strategic, operating like hunters in a crowded market. They scan for the biggest, loudest, most visible and vulnerable targets and identify the cases they can close quickly. If you're small and under the radar, they might pass you by, simply because they didn't see you. Start growing fast, expanding into new territories, grabbing headlines and making noise and you're lighting yourself up like a Christmas tree.

Enforcement is not just about non-compliance, it is about visibility, vulnerability and volume. This is where the Enforcement Risk Radar comes in. This tool does not tell you whether you are compliant – that is the job of your documentation, risk assessments, technical files and internal audits – instead it tells you how likely you are to show up on the radar of enforcement bodies in the UK and EU. This is your enforcement profile; your operational footprint in the eyes of regulators. Whether you realise it or not, enforcement bodies are constantly scanning for companies that hit the patterns this radar identifies.

This is the paradox: being compliant doesn't stop you from showing up on the radar, what it does is stop what happens next. Visibility leads to scrutiny, scrutiny leads to questions and if your answers aren't solid, investigation and enforcement follow.

The purpose of the radar

I created the Enforcement Risk Radar to help clients stop playing regulatory roulette. It answers the key questions: How brightly are you going to appear on the radar in the first place? How big is your brand signature?

How the radar works

The radar is built around six core risk zones, each one directly influencing how visible you are to enforcement. It's not about whether you're doing things intentionally wrong, it's about how the size, shape and behaviour of your business increases the chance that a regulator notices you.

If you are more visible, with more locations, markets, SKUs and cross-border activity, the radar lights up. If you've had enforcement action before, the radar and regulators remember.

This tool gives you a score based on the combined weight of your activity across these six factors.

A note on scope

This scoring system applies specifically to the UK and EU member states. It reflects how Trading Standards, the Office for Product Safety and Standards (OPSS) in the UK and equivalent EU enforcement agencies actually behave.

It reflects the unique structure of European market enforcement, which is fragmented, varies by country and often operates at the local authority level, not just nationally. It does not necessarily apply to the United States, Canada, Australia or other regions, although the principles involved may well be carried through on some level.

The six core risk zones

No matter your sector – cosmetics, adult toys, PPE, consumer electronics, toys or novel nicotine – the same visibility principles apply. If you don't know what triggers attention, you can't manage it. The following six risk zones highlight where enforcement risk comes from.

1. The visibility multiplier

The first risk zone is the number of locations your products are sold in. Every additional retail shelf is another exposure point. Every time you expand into a new store, you increase the number of eyes – good and bad – on your brand.

The most dangerous channels are independent shops, market stalls and non-chain retailers.

These environments often have little regulatory oversight, inconsistent supply chains and poor compliance hygiene. They are catnip for inspectors because they know they're more likely to uncover counterfeit goods, unsafe products or dodgy paperwork there. If your product is sitting on those shelves, you're part of the sweep whether you like it or not.

Here's the kicker: You might be fully compliant but if your retailers aren't, you still get hit. Regulators don't always differentiate between the manufacturer and the seller when they seize products or issue penalties.

The trap: Believing that more stockists automatically equals more success.

The reality: More visibility equals more exposure and, in some cases, more risk than reward.

2. Previous enforcement exposure

Welcome to the watchlist. Had a warning letter? A product seizure? Even just a 'guidance call' from an official? Congratulations, you're on file.

Your company and product names are now searchable in enforcement systems. That means the next time an inspector is scanning for issues in your sector, your name pops up as a 'known entity'. Second checks happen faster, tolerance for mistakes drops and follow-ups are expected.

This isn't paranoia, it's a process. Regulators operate like any other organisation with finite resources: they prioritise businesses they've already touched because they're easier to justify revisiting.

The trap: Thinking enforcement is a one-off.

The reality: Once they know who you are, you stay on their radar for years.

3. Number of markets sold into

Next up is the number of markets you sell into. Each country has its own enforcement culture, and it's rarely uniform across a region. Some countries are aggressive and proactive (think Germany, France and Poland), some seem passive until a complaint lands (for example, Malta and Cyprus) and others are strict, inflexible and quick to penalise (such as Switzerland and Norway).

Founders often believe that 'EU compliant' means they're safe everywhere in Europe. That's a dangerous assumption. Even within the EU single market, enforcement practices vary wildly from one country to the next.

The trap: Believing compliance certificates automatically travel with your product.

The reality: Every new market comes with new enforcement rules and fresh exposure.

4. Cross-border or distance sales

Selling into countries where you lack a local presence, a responsible person (RP) or an authorised representative (AR)? That's a flashing enforcement target.

Inspectors increasingly order products online, test shipping destinations and use those transactions as triggers for investigation. They're not just playing catch-up; they're actively scanning e-commerce flows to spot breaches of local regulations.

One founder I spoke with thought their e-commerce site was 'borderless' until regulators in France placed a test order and used it to block their entire product range from entry.

The trap: Assuming online sales are invisible.

The reality: Every cross-border delivery into a restricted country is a potential violation.

5. Lack of an RP or AR

Trying to sell in the UK or EU without the legally appointed RP or AR? That's a non-compliance red flag.

This is often the first question regulators ask when they audit a product. If you don't have one, the process usually stops right there. Seizures, penalties and delistings often follow immediately.

Many founders treat the RP or AR as an optional administrative task. It's not. It's the gatekeeper for accessing regulated markets, and the absence of one tells regulators you don't understand (or care about) the basics.

The trap: Thinking you can delay appointing an RP or AR 'until we grow a bit more'.

The reality: This is one of the fastest ways to get flagged before you've even scaled.

6. Number of SKUs or product variants

Every SKU needs its own documentation. Labels, claims, formulations, testing records, it all has to be correct and up to date.

As your catalogue grows, so does the complexity of managing compliance. More products equals more points of failure. One bad label across fifty SKUs isn't just a single mistake, it's fifty violations, multiplied across every market and retailer you serve.

I've seen fast-growing brands stumble because they assumed their old systems would scale with them. They didn't.

The trap: Believing growth solves all problems.

The reality: Growth without structure equals risk without limits.

Enforcement targets the easy wins

Regulators aren't out to get you but they are under pressure. They need quick victories and they want the highest-impact, lowest-effort targets so they go after highly visible brands, poorly documented products, repeat offenders and cross-border sales with no representation.

How to use the Enforcement Risk Radar

The Enforcement Risk Radar isn't just a concept, it's a tool; a way for you to see your business the way regulators do and take action before they do. Here's a six-step guide to how to use it:

1. Map your exposure: Where are your products showing up?

Start by tracing every channel where your products are visible. Not just the big retailers you supply directly but also the smaller outlets, online resellers and even grey-market distributors you might not know about.

Every additional retail shelf is a potential exposure point. Independent shops, market stalls and discount stores are particularly risky. They tend to have weak compliance practices, making them magnets for inspections.

Founders often assume, 'If I didn't put it there, it's not my responsibility.' Regulators disagree. If your name is on the label, you're in the frame.

Action: Ask yourself: 'Could my products be swept up in an enforcement raid simply because of where they're sold?'

2. Review your compliance history: Have you been flagged before?

Think back. Has your company ever received a warning letter, had a shipment seized or even been contacted for 'advice' by regulators? If so, congratulations: you're on their watchlist. Your company and product names are now logged in enforcement systems. This makes you a known entity. Next time, they won't hesitate to run your name through their database or revisit your case.

Action: Pull out any previous correspondence or reports and check whether the issues were fully resolved or if they left lingering weaknesses that regulators might revisit.

3. Check your markets: Are you selling into risky jurisdictions without support?

Founders often assume that if their product is 'EU compliant', they're safe everywhere. This is a dangerous myth.

Action: Audit where you're selling and ask: 'Do I understand the enforcement priorities in each country?' 'Do I have local expertise or representation to manage them?'

4. Audit your distance selling: Are you shipping into countries where it's restricted?

Cross-border e-commerce can be a compliance minefield. Selling into countries where you lack a local RP or AR is a red flag. Regulators are increasingly ordering products online and testing shipping destinations to catch out brands.

Action: Ask yourself: 'Are we accidentally breaching regulations every time an order comes through our website?' If you're not sure, it's time to review your e-commerce flows before they light you up on the radar.

5. Triage your SKUs: Are they all documented and up to date?

Every SKU represents a point of compliance risk. Labels, claims, certifications and technical files need to be accurate and current.

As your product range grows, so does the likelihood of errors creeping in. One mislabelled product doesn't just create a single problem, it multiplies across every market and retailer it touches.

Founders often assume their old systems will scale as they grow. In reality, scaling without structure creates risk without limits.

Action: Review your product catalogue and flag any SKUs lacking full documentation.

6. Clean your retail network: Are third parties putting you at risk?

Inspectors love to target retailers with poor compliance hygiene. If your products are stocked by third parties who cut corners, you get dragged into their mess.

Ask yourself: 'Are my distributors, stockists and retail partners following the rules or are they creating enforcement magnets?' One founder I worked with had flawless products but still ended up in hot water because a reseller had altered their packaging.

Regulators didn't care who made the change; the brand took the hit.

Action: Clean your retail network and cut ties with partners who won't step up.

Why this matters

The Enforcement Risk Radar helps you see what inspectors see. It's not enough to stay compliant, you also need to avoid looking non-compliant. The more you understand how these six risk zones work together, the better equipped you are to operate confidently in regulated markets.

Scoring the six risk zones

This is not a paper exercise. It is designed as a live scoring system built directly into the ARC platform. As your business changes – adding SKUs, expanding markets, increasing retail footprint, resolving or triggering enforcement events – your score will change.

It becomes part of your ongoing compliance health check. It's not static, but moves with your business.

1. Number of locations

The more locations your products are marketed in, the higher your exposure to enforcement.

Independent retailers are particularly high risk because they often lack internal compliance teams. Regulators routinely inspect small retailers looking for easy enforcement wins.

Selling through large chains does not remove the risk entirely, it changes the nature of the risk. Large chains tend to require stronger documentation upfront, but once you are in the enforcement, checks happen more at the supply chain level than the store level.

Scoring

- **1 point:** 1–500 locations
- **2 points:** 501–1,000 locations
- **3 points:** 1,001–5,000 locations
- **4 points:** 5,001–10,000 locations
- **5 points:** Over 10,000 locations

2. Previous enforcement exposure

Once you're on a regulator's radar, you stay there.

A single guidance meeting raises your profile. A warning letter, seizure or RAPEX (EU Safety Gate) notification escalates it further. Regulators share information between departments, between countries and even across regulatory sectors.

If you have a history, you are no longer anonymous. Follow-up checks become faster, tolerance for error drops and your name gets circulated.

Scoring

- **1 point:** Guidance meeting
- **2 points:** Warning letter
- **3 points:** Product seizure
- **4 points:** RAPEX or other safety alert
- **5 points:** Enforced product recall

3. Number of markets sold into

Every market is a new set of eyes on your products.

Each country has its own enforcement agencies, its own approach to compliance and its own risk tolerance. Some countries are highly active (for example Germany, France, the Nordics), while others are more reactive, but every border crossed means a new regulator scanning products for issues.

The complexity compounds rapidly. Labels, documentation, translations and responsible entities all multiply with each market.

Scoring

- **1 point:** 1–6 markets
- **2 points:** 7–12 markets
- **3 points:** 13–17 markets
- **4 points:** 18–22 markets
- **5 points:** 23–28 markets

4. Cross-border or distance sales

Cross-border sales are one of the biggest visibility triggers for enforcement agencies. Regulators routinely perform test purchases online to check whether restricted products are being shipped illegally into their jurisdiction.

If you allow unrestricted distance sales, especially without tight contractual controls, you are lighting up on the radar. This is one of the fastest ways to invite enforcement scrutiny, particularly in sectors like novel nicotine, cosmetics, adult products and medical devices, where cross-border rules vary widely.

Scoring

- **1 point:** No cross-border sales, contracts in place to prevent it

- **2 points:** No cross-border sales allowed, but no contracts in place

- **3 points:** Cross-border allowed with robust geographic contracts

- **4 points:** Cross-border allowed with only verbal agreements

- **5 points:** Cross-border allowed freely with no restrictions

5. Lack of an of RP or AR

This is one of the first and easiest checks that enforcement bodies run. No RP or AR? You are instantly non-compliant for that market. Having an informal, verbal or shell-company arrangement does not hold water with regulators, especially in the EU and UK.

This is a clear-cut, binary compliance trigger. Enforcement agencies love this check because it is simple, fast and easy to enforce.

Scoring

- **1 point:** Formal RP or AR appointed, contracts in place, fully compliant

- **2 points:** RP or AR role filled by distributor without full documentation

- **3 points:** Informal RP or AR arrangement without clear obligations

- **4 points:** Self-appointed RP via shell or virtual company

- **5 points:** No RP or AR appointed for any market

6. Number of SKUs or product variants

Every SKU multiplies compliance complexity. Each product requires a technical file, safety assessment, labelling review, claims check and traceable documentation. The higher the SKU count, the more likely an error slips through: a missed label update, an expired test report or a documentation gap.

SKU volume without matching system maturity is one of the fastest ways to trigger enforcement action.

Scoring

- **1 point:** 1–10 SKUs

- **2 points:** 11–25 SKUs

- **3 points:** 26–50 SKUs

- **4 points:** 51–100 SKUs

- **5 points:** Over 100 SKUs

How to use this score

This is not about guessing or gut feel, but is a diagnostic tool that tells you where you sit on the radar today.

- **Low score** = Lower visibility, lower enforcement risk

- **High score** = High visibility, high probability of scrutiny

This does not predict compliance. A brand with a high radar score but bulletproof systems and a strong compliance culture may withstand scrutiny just fine. But a brand with a high radar score and weak systems? That is where enforcement bites, fast, hard and with little warning.

How to stay off the radar

Here's the uncomfortable truth: You can't erase every risk. No matter how tight your systems, there will always be variables outside your control, market shifts, partner mistakes or enforcement officers with quotas to hit. What you can do is close the obvious gaps, fix the vulnerabilities that regulators look for first and make your brand less visible to the wrong people. Think of it like a house with a 'beware of the dog' sign. The dog doesn't have to be perfect, it just has to make the inspector think twice before knocking on your door.

Appoint a credible RP or AR

In the UK and EU, your RP or AR is the first thing regulators check. If you don't have one or if the one you've appointed is little more than a name on a piece of paper, you're waving a red flag.

Appointing a credible RP/AR sends a very different signal: 'This company understands the rules. This company is serious.' It's not just about meeting legal requirements; it's about showing you're not an easy target.

Patch the distance-selling loopholes

Cross-border e-commerce has created a new compliance minefield. Regulators are actively placing test orders, tracking shipments and using them to build enforcement cases.

Audit your online store. Are you shipping into countries where you lack representation? Are you complying with local labelling laws and consumer protection rules? If not, you're lighting yourself up. Fix it now, before an inspector finds you through their own shopping cart.

Retire high-risk SKUs if the documentation isn't solid

Sometimes the boldest move is to hit pause.

If a product's technical documentation is incomplete or out of date, it's a liability. One bad SKU can contaminate your whole range in the eyes of regulators.

Retiring or reformulating these products doesn't mean you're giving up. It means you're protecting the credibility of your entire brand while you regroup and strengthen.

Fix anything that previously triggered enforcement

If you've been flagged before, you're already on the watchlist. Go back over the issues. Did you resolve them fully or just put a sticking plaster on top? Regulators don't forget, and they'll often revisit previous offenders to check progress.

Proactive founders take away the temptation. They fix the original problem so thoroughly that even the most cynical inspector has nothing to criticise.

Audit your retailer network for weak links

Your compliance is only as strong as the weakest partner in your supply chain. If third-party retailers are cutting corners, altering packaging, selling into restricted markets or stocking counterfeit variants, you're the one who gets the knock on the door.

Audit your network, educate your partners and don't be afraid to cut ties with those who won't step up. It's better to lose a few sales than to lose your reputation.

The goal

This isn't about creating a perfect, airtight operation. That doesn't exist. It's about becoming the kind of company regulators scroll past on their radar. It's about sending every signal that says: 'We're not worth the hassle. Look elsewhere.'

In a world where enforcement resources are limited, that mindset shift can make all the difference.

Final word

This is the real-world pattern of how enforcement works in regulated markets. It's not about luck. It's not even strictly about whether your product is compliant. It's about visibility, pressure and whether you look like an easy win for overworked enforcement teams trying to make their numbers.

The Enforcement Risk Radar shows you how bright your signal is and how regulators see your brand as they scan for their next target. Seeing the signal isn't enough; if you don't have strong systems and a culture that takes compliance seriously, the first knock on the door can turn into an existential crisis. This radar is not there to scare you. It is there to give you control.

Regulators are using their own invisible radar. This is yours. Know your score, what it means, where the weak spots are and where to focus next because in this game, what you cannot see will hurt you.

That's where the ARC methodology comes in. It's your defensive shield, your structural advantage and your accelerator, all rolled into one. ARC isn't just about staying alive; it's about staying ahead because in regulated markets, the founders who master compliance don't just survive, they thrive, while others stall.

This is how you stop being a target and start being untouchable.

10
Compliance As A
Growth Engine

M ost founders still see compliance as something boring and painful, a box-ticking exercise designed to keep regulators away and avoid fines. Investors do not see it that way – not even close. For them, compliance is not about staying out of trouble, it is about reducing risk, increasing scalability and building a business that can withstand scrutiny from every angle. It becomes a signal of operational maturity and credibility, the difference between a deal that excites investors and one that quietly dies in due diligence.

This chapter will show you why compliance is not just a regulatory obligation but an investable asset. It will help you see the link between audit-ready systems and higher valuations, between risk management and deal velocity. Because in regulated markets, founders who treat compliance like strategy don't just survive, they win.

What investor-ready compliance really means

If you are raising capital, planning an exit or entering a new partnership, you need more than a great growth story. You must prove beyond a shadow of doubt that your business can operate safely, legally and without disruption in every market you serve. This is where investor-ready compliance becomes mission-critical.

It means you are prepared for someone to lift the hood of your business, poke around in every corner and find nothing that scares them. No hidden regulatory liabilities, no 'we thought the manufacturer handled that' surprises, no last-minute scrambles to find expired certificates or missing technical files. It means you are not just operating, you are audit-ready, scale-ready and exit-ready.

Investors do not expect zero risk; that is a fantasy. What they expect is that you understand your risk, own it and are actively managing it.

What investors look for

Investors don't want vague reassurances or verbal promises. They are looking for evidence by hunting for the following signals.

1. A systematic approach

Compliance cannot be a one-time project or 'something we check when there's an issue'.

Is there a structured methodology in place, like ARC? Are your core compliance workflows real, documented and operational? Are you using platforms like MAVRYX and VIGIL to embed compliance in day-to-day operations?

The system matters more than the size of your compliance team. Investors want to know the machine runs, even when the founder is not pushing every button.

Red flag: 'We've got it in a spreadsheet somewhere.'

Green flag: 'Here's the system, here's the dashboard, here's how we track and update risk weekly.'

2. Documented, complete technical files

This is non-negotiable. For every product you sell, you must be able to show:

- A full, current and correct technical file (depending on the industry and/or product, the complexity of this file will change)

- Safety assessments and lab testing reports

- Certificates of conformity and market-specific authorisations

- Reviewed labels and packaging files

- RP appointments, where required

If even one product is missing, it becomes a liability. Investors spot it, lawyers flag it and deals stall or collapse.

In one recent case, a promising cosmetics brand lost a major investment because two of their top-selling SKUs lacked updated Declarations of Conformity. Everything else in their pitch was solid, but that one gap raised doubts about their operational maturity and risked future enforcement issues.

3. Active PMS

Investors hate surprises. PMS proves you are learning from the market instead of waiting for enforcement to teach you the hard way.

Are you tracking complaints, returns and safety issues? Are those events logged, risk assessed and actioned? Does your PMS process feed back into product updates and risk registers? This is how you show investors you are not blind to the real-world performance of your products.

Brands using scalable software for live complaint tracking and trend analysis often breeze through due diligence. They can demonstrate a closed-loop process where issues are caught early, investigated and resolved – exactly the kind of operational discipline investors value.

4. Clear ownership and accountability

Who owns compliance inside your business? Even if you are small, someone must be visibly and explicitly accountable. Investors hate discovering that compliance is 'sort of everyone's job', which is code for 'no one's job'.

Bonus points: If that person has access to the right tools, runs regular compliance reviews and is backed by external advisers, you immediately look more investable.

5. Scalable market access plans

Growth into new markets excites investors, until they realise you are not legally allowed to sell there.

Who is your RP in the EU? How do you plan to manage UK compliance? What's your strategy for multi-country label compliance? If you have clear, documented market access plans – not just a commercial strategy but a regulatory one – investors breathe easier.

The founder mindset shift

Being investor-ready is the same as being audit-ready. It is not something you scramble to patch together when due diligence kicks off, it is how professional founders operate by default.

The founders who secure the best deals, the cleanest raises, the fastest exits, the highest multiples are the ones who can say, without hesitation: 'Yes, we have got that covered and here is the evidence.'

They do not say it with bravado. They say it with:

- A digital file
- A signed declaration
- A risk register with real data
- A MAVRYX dashboard that provides systems, not guesswork

Risk-protected IP: The hidden value most founders ignore

When most people hear 'intellectual property', they think of patents, trademarks, copyrights, formulas and logos. In regulated industries, where products touch skin, go into lungs, enter the body or are designed to protect lives, the real IP extends far beyond that. Your risk management systems, safety data, compliance records and technical files are intellectual property too.

Not just admin IP but valuable, commercially powerful IP that drives valuation.

Why risk-protected IP matters

The better you manage risk, the more valuable this hidden IP becomes. It protects you from fines, enforcement, delisting and recall. It makes your products defensible and your systems scalable. It makes your business more attractive to investors, acquirers and retail partners.

Risk mitigation is not just defensive, it is offensive. It is a value driver. It is commercial leverage.

Four ways risk mitigation strengthens your IP and valuation

1. Technical files = proof of process. Safety testing, formulations, product specs, Declarations of Conformity and RP appointments prove that you are a professional operator.

2. Claims that are built to last. When marketing claims are backed by lab tests and scientific data, they stop being fragile. Documented brands win.

3. Systemised documentation is portable IP. When compliance lives in a system like MAVRYX or VIGIL, it becomes operational IP; repeatable, transferable, defensible.

4. Training, SOPs and repeatability = enterprise-grade IP. If your compliance knowledge only lives in your head, it is a liability, but if it is documented, trained and embedded across your team, you have built something bigger than yourself.

Final word

Risk mitigation does not just reduce the chance of failure, it directly increases the probability of success.

When you treat compliance systems, risk registers and technical documentation as IP (not admin), you change the value of your business. You become more investable, more scalable, harder to copy and harder to displace.

The rule is simple: If it is not documented, it does not exist. If it is not systemised, it is not scalable. If it is not owned, it is a liability.

Stop treating compliance like an annoying side quest. Treat it like finance, operations or marketing – like the line on your valuation that it actually is. When the time comes to raise, expand or exit, the founders who own their compliance walk in with power and walk out with better deals. Every single time.

11
The Enforcement Landscape

We are living through the biggest enforcement shift in decades. Welcome to the new age of compliance policing.

Enforcement is up and it's getting smarter. In 2024 alone, the EU Safety Gate (formerly RAPEX) logged over 25,000 alerts for non-food consumer products, and that number continues to grow each quarter. In fact, Q1 2025 saw 3,925 separate product recall events across key sectors, marking the most active quarter in eleven years.

This is not theory, it's reality. Authorities are not just reacting to incidents anymore; they're actively hunting for non-compliant products using a mix of AI tools, data scraping and marketplace surveillance.

Enforcement is happening faster, earlier and further upstream than ever before.

A sector-by-sector snapshot

Gone are the days when enforcement meant a surprise visit from a human inspector, clipboard in hand. Today, regulators are becoming more digital, aggressive and proactive, especially in the UK and EU. If you're operating in regulated sectors like novel nicotine, cosmetics, toys, PPE, consumer electronics or adult products, the enforcement landscape has changed beneath your feet. Let's look at each of these sectors in turn.

Novel nicotine

Regulators across the UK and EU are stepping up scrutiny after the Tobacco Products Directive (an EU law). Local Trading Standards teams in the UK are backed by central OPSS enforcement support, and retailers are now receiving direct enforcement notices, not just manufacturers.

The most common triggers for enforcement in novel nicotine are:

- Non-compliant tank sizes and nicotine strengths

- Packaging breaches (especially misused health warnings or missing ingredients)

- Grey imports not properly notified to MHRA or the relevant EU databases

Recent cases have shown entire shipments seized at ports and products removed from marketplaces like Amazon and eBay before they even reach consumers, based purely on algorithmic label checks and barcode screening.

Cosmetics

The cosmetic sector is now one of the most active for recalls and RAPEX listings in the EU.

Frequent violations include:

- Missing or incorrect Product Information Files (PIFs)

- Undeclared allergens or restricted substances

- Incomplete labelling or absent RP declarations

Authorities are relying heavily on market surveillance and whistleblowing via consumer complaints and competitor reports. With AI now scanning websites and e-commerce platforms for keywords and claim violations, expect enforcement to hit sooner and harder.

Toys and children's products

Toy recalls continue to dominate EU Safety Gate reports. Common failures include:

- Choking hazards from detachable parts
- Inadequate CE or UKCA documentation
- Incomplete safety assessments or traceability gaps

UK Trading Standards and EU authorities are particularly aggressive in this space. Many toy sellers importing via China or dropshipping platforms are getting caught out due to documentation that's either missing or doesn't stand up to audit.

Personal Protective Equipment

Since COVID-19, PPE enforcement remains heightened. The EU and UK authorities are still cracking down on:

- False claims of certification (especially misused CE or UKCA marks)
- Expired or unverified test reports
- Mislabelled or unaudited import routes

Recent recalls include face masks, gloves and eye protection gear flagged for inadequate filtration or fraudulent conformity documentation. Expect regulators to treat all PPE as high risk until proven otherwise.

Electrical and electronics

This is a massive area for enforcement across both the UK and EU.

Common pitfalls include:

- Incomplete technical documentation
- Absence of Declaration of Conformity
- Failure to meet Restriction of Hazardous Substances (RoHS) or electronic medicines compendium (EMC) standards
- Unsafe chargers, batteries or plug adaptors

E-commerce platforms like Amazon now require full compliance documentation before listing, and regulators are increasingly partnering with platforms to trigger proactive delistings, with no notice and no appeal.

Adult products

This category is now seeing spillover enforcement from cosmetics and electronics, especially where items fall under dual classifications (e.g. vibrating devices, smart apps or electrical heating elements).

Issues that trigger action include:

- No CE or UKCA marking
- Battery overheating or electrical risk
- Labelling that fails basic safety communication standards

As mainstream retailers move into adult wellness, regulators are no longer ignoring this category. Enforcement is being driven both by safety concerns and increasing scrutiny around materials, allergens and marketing claims.

The rise of AI-driven enforcement

One of the most important shifts is where enforcement happens.

Traditionally, compliance checks took place at ports of entry, in-person inspections and post-incident investigations. Now, enforcement is starting before the product enters the country (via advance declaration checks), at the point of listing on e-commerce platforms (automated compliance scans) and during routine algorithmic sweeps of packaging photos, product pages and marketing copy.

Expect more:

- Digital 'compliance crawlers' scanning marketplaces for claim violations or missing symbols

- Barcode tracking systems verifying declarations before products can be shipped

- Real-time flagging of non-conformities from consumer photos and complaints submitted online

AI isn't replacing human enforcement, it's amplifying it.

Final word

Regulators are watching, enforcement is happening and in every one of your sectors, the rules are getting tighter, smarter and less forgiving.

You're not just being judged on whether you've done the paperwork. You're being judged on whether your entire operational model is built to stay ahead of risk, not scramble after it.

If your compliance strategy hasn't been reviewed recently, or if it still relies on reactive processes and gut instinct, it's time for a rethink.

The enforcement landscape is no longer a background concern, it's the battlefield.

12
Digital Product Passports

I magine a world where every product has a digital DNA: an uneditable, scannable trail of where it came from, what it's made of, who touched it, how it was tested and when it went to market. This isn't sci-fi, this is Digital Product Passports (DPPs), and they're about to change compliance forever.

Since 2017, I've been banging the drum about the importance of documentation, traceability and real-time oversight. For a long time, it felt like we were shouting into the void, but now the EU has drawn a line in the sand and the entire supply chain is being forced to listen.

What is a Digital Product Passport?

A DPP is a structured, machine-readable digital record that follows a product throughout its lifecycle, from design and manufacture to retail, repair, reuse and recycling.

Each passport contains a full data record, including:

- Unique product identifiers

- Materials and substances used

- Compliance certifications

- Sustainability and repairability info

- Manufacturer, importer and UKRP/EUAR data

- Evidence of conformity with EU regulations

- Lists of standards applied, commodity codes, EU legislation/directives and regulations

The list goes on. This isn't a PDF uploaded to a dusty portal, this is live, linked, interoperable data, designed to be accessed by regulators, customs authorities, consumers and other businesses at the tap of a device.

DPPs are coming first to high-impact sectors like textiles, batteries and electronics, but the scope will expand. If you're in novel nicotine, toys, cosmetics, PPE and the adult toy industry, it's not a matter of if, it's when.

Why DPPs change the game

Let's be blunt. The old compliance model was flawed: paper-based, easy to fake, easy to hide. Brands could bluff, traders could lie, enforcement was hit-and-miss.

DPPs blow that world apart. Every product will need its paperwork *before* it hits the shelf – not when it's requested or when something goes wrong, but before – every time. It will travel with the product and be readable, wherever it goes. You either have it or you don't. You're either clean or you're exposed.

Once DPPs are mandatory, hiding behind offshore ownership structures or shell brands won't work. Every actor in the supply chain becomes visible – and accountable.

AI + DPPs = total transparency

When we pair DPPs with AI-powered regulatory investigations, that's where things get nuclear.

Regulators will use technology and artificial intelligence to:

- Scan millions of products instantly (Rain RFID will see to that)
- Cross-reference supplier declarations and conformity documents

- Flag inconsistencies in real time

- Detect copy-paste certificates, fake lab reports and greenwashing

Customs agents and online marketplaces will have AI tools that can instantly verify whether a product's DPP checks out. The moment something looks fishy – a wrong material code, expired test report or missing SDS – a red flag goes up.

This isn't manual spot checks anymore, it's systemic surveillance. Bad actors won't just get fined, they'll get shut down, blacklisted, swept off Amazon, wiped from Shopify and dropped by every responsible retailer.

Why good brands should celebrate

If that makes you nervous, good – it means you're not a fraud. For legitimate, founder-led brands, this is your moment. You've been doing the hard work, building transparent supply chains, working with certified labs, keeping your documents in order and caring about what goes in and on your product. Now you finally get the competitive advantage you deserve.

In a world of DPPs, trust is trackable. Your reputation is no longer based on marketing, it's backed by metadata. That's the compliance edge.

Final word

This is the last era of hiding. When DPPs become the norm, you won't be able to duck inspections, outsource responsibility to shady suppliers or stall for time while you 'chase your documents'. You'll either have the data at your fingertips or you'll be out of the market.

The age of plausible deniability is over. This is the age of total traceability.

If you're a founder who's doing the right thing, good. You're about to punch above your weight. You'll win trust faster, sell in more countries and avoid regulatory landmines before they explode.

If you're still winging it? Still hoping no one notices? DPPs are coming and they're bringing receipts.

13
The Loophole Loop

In regulated markets, there's a game being played every single day and it's not on a level playing field. On one side, you've got the regulators – bureaucratic, cautious, armed with statutes and enforcement teams, convinced they're protecting the public from harm. On the other side, you've got founders – scrappy, fast-moving and driven by vision and survival instincts. This isn't just competition, this is war.

The truth? Entrepreneurs innovate faster than regulators can draft consultation papers. When new rules finally arrive, those same founders have already pivoted, sidestepped or launched something completely new.

This dance between innovation and regulation creates a repeating cycle, which I call the loophole loop. If you're building a business in a regulated industry, you're either running inside this loop or trying to escape it.

1. Innovation
2. Regulation
3. Circumvention
4. Enforcement

The loophole loop: A game of cat and mouse played between entrepreneurs and enforcement agencies

Innovation outruns the rulebook

Founders see opportunity where others see risk.

In emerging sectors like vaping, cannabis, CBD and even adult toys, the rules often start vague or non-existent. Entrepreneurs take advantage of this head start to build markets and generate demand before the authorities even realise what's happening.

Take the early vape industry. When regulators clamped down on nicotine-containing e-liquids, smart entrepreneurs didn't panic, they pivoted. They launched 'short-fills' – nicotine-free liquids sold in oversized bottles, leaving space for customers to add a separate nicotine shot themselves. No nicotine, no regulation – at least for a while.

This isn't unique to vapes. In the cannabis world, CBD products exploded in popularity while regulators struggled to classify them. Founders exploited this grey zone, launching everything from oils to gummies without clear oversight.

At this stage, innovation thrives unchecked. Founders love this part of the game – it feels rebellious, exciting and with high rewards.

The regulator awakens

Nothing stays unregulated forever. As markets grow so does public attention. Media stories emerge about dodgy products, safety concerns or outright scandals and politicians start asking questions. Regulators are pressured to 'do something'.

This is where frameworks get drafted, categories defined and boundaries drawn. But enforcement? That's another story. Drafting laws, consulting stakeholders and pushing rules through the political machine takes time, sometimes years. For founders, this lag time is golden.

The founder's sidestep

Savvy entrepreneurs don't wait around for the hammer to fall. They adapt, they pivot, they innovate again. Here's how they do it:

- **Regulatory arbitrage.** Selling in jurisdictions with weak or non-existent enforcement.

- **Product reclassification.** Positioning products in categories outside regulatory scope. (CBD sold as a cosmetic instead of a food supplement, for example.)

- **Component separation.** Breaking regulated elements into separate parts. (Vape kits sold without nicotine; nicotine sold separately.)

- **Timing launches.** Moving fast before legislation catches up.

Every time the net tightens, founders are already one step ahead, building their next move.

When the net tightens

Eventually, the game changes. Authorities catch up, loopholes close, definitions broaden and penalties increase. The grey market that once seemed limitless now faces raids, fines and even criminal charges.

We've seen this story repeat with vape shops fined for exceeding nicotine limits, CBD businesses forced to pull products after novel food rulings and cannabis operators shut down for exploiting legal grey areas.

At this point, only two kinds of companies survive:

1. **The proactive compliant.** Those who saw the crackdown coming and got their house in order early.

2. **The legal brawler.** Those with deep enough pockets to fight regulators in court.

The rest? They vanish.

The loophole loop in full

This isn't a one-time event, it's a cycle:

Innovation → Regulation → Circumvention → Enforcement → Repeat

Founders innovate, regulators react, entrepreneurs pivot, authorities tighten the net, and around it goes.

In industries like vaping, cannabis and consumer tech, this loop has lasted for decades, but here's the catch: Every cycle carries more risk than the last.

The founder's dilemma

For founders in regulated markets, the temptation to play the loophole game is strong. It's faster, it's cheaper, it feels entrepreneurial, but it's also a gamble.

Every loophole has a shelf life, every sidestep increases exposure and when regulators finally close the net, the penalties can wipe out years of hard work overnight.

At some point, every founder faces a choice: Keep dodging rules until you get caught or turn compliance into a *competitive weapon*.

Compliance as a moat

The companies that thrive in regulated markets aren't the ones with the best loophole strategies. They're the ones who break free from the cycle and use compliance to build a moat around their business.

A moat:

- Keeps competitors at bay
- Makes you untouchable to regulators
- Builds trust with customers and investors alike

In regulated markets, compliance isn't just ticking boxes, it's a barrier to entry – a growth accelerator. It's how you stop playing the cat-and-mouse game and start dominating your market.

Here's the real question: Are you still running in the loophole loop or are you ready to build a fortress around your brand?

A word to founders

If you're building a business in a regulated sector, this is not a drill. You're playing the game on hard mode. Everywhere you look, the walls are closing in. Rules are tightening, enforcement teams are scaling, and retailers and marketplaces are shifting the burden of proof squarely on to you. The days of 'we didn't know' or 'nobody told us' are over.

One founder I spoke to recently summed it up perfectly when they said: 'I feel like we're sprinting up an escalator that's going down, and now someone's cranked the speed up.'

Here's the brutal truth: If you're only aiming to *survive*, you've already lost. If you're just dodging bullets and crossing your fingers that the next warning letter lands on someone else's desk, you're one compliance failure away from collapse.

What do you do? You *lead*. Not just internally, not just for your team. You become the brand regulators respect, retailers trust and competitors can't keep up with. Here's how.

The no-excuses checklist

Let's strip it down to what serious operators are doing right now:

- **You have a live, visible and prioritised risk register.** No more dusty spreadsheets buried on someone's laptop. No more 'I think we're covered'. Every credible founder I know can pull up a single page showing where the risks are, who owns them and what's being done about them.

- **You have agile systems in place.** Version control, change control, real-time documentation. It doesn't matter if you're a five-person start-up or a 500-person scale-up, if your systems can't flex and adapt as regulations evolve, you're building on quicksand.

- **You have a compliance culture from top to bottom.** This isn't about hiring a compliance manager and pretending the job is done. Founders who win make compliance part of every conversation, from marketing to logistics to R&D.

- **You build packaging reviews into your launch process.** A client of mine once lost an entire shipment because of a single missing CE mark on packaging. Now every claim, label and symbol is checked before it hits the shelf.

- **You track regulatory change in every market you operate in.** Not via Google Alerts or by accident but proactively and systematically.

- **You treat complaints, incidents and feedback as fuel for improvement.** The founders who thrive use PMS as their early warning system, spotting trends and fixing root causes before they become scandals.

- **You stop seeing compliance as a cost.** This isn't admin, it's your moat, your edge, your accelerator.

If you don't have these systems in place, start now. If you do, tighten, test and evolve them.

The founder's mindset that wins

Here's what I've noticed: The founders who win in regulated sectors are not the most technical or the ones who outsource everything and hope it works out, they are the ones who *own it*.

They understand that credibility is earned, not claimed; growth without control is a liability; and chaos kills momentum.

Here's the mindset shift: Stop seeing compliance as something to survive. Start seeing it as something to master. Master it and your launches are faster, your investors are calmer, your retailers are stickier, your team runs without drama and you sleep at night.

The alternative? A slow drift toward enforcement, burnout and breakdown.

You didn't start this business to babysit documents, you started it to build something that lasts. This is how you make that happen.

TRUE STORY: How compliance became a secret weapon for an adult toy brand

Recently, we started working with a fast-growing adult toy company – let's call them Pulse & Bloom. Female-founded, inclusive and focused on sexual wellness with a sustainability edge, they weren't new to the scene. Online they were thriving, but every time they tried to step up to land shelf space in pharmacies or department stores across the UK and Europe, they hit the same wall. Buyers were interested but legal teams said no.

The problem was compliance credibility. There's no single product-specific regulation for adult toys in the UK or EU. Instead, brands have to navigate a patchwork of general safety requirements from the General Product Safety Regulation (GPSR), cosmetics regulations (depending on the product) and RoHS (depending on the product), to CE marking, electrical safety and risk-based documentation. Most companies fudge it with vague lab tests and Declarations of Conformity that don't stack up, or simply hope no one asks.

Pulse & Bloom wanted to be different. They didn't just want to appear compliant; they wanted to lead with it. That's when we introduced them to the ARC methodology:

1. **Agile systems.** We helped them build a lightweight but structured compliance system from the inside out. Even with a modest range of SKUs, they were planning for scale so their systems had to keep up. We mapped their product journey and embedded key compliance checkpoints: during product development, before packaging was finalised and before launch. Technical files were brought up to spec – nothing excessive, just sharp, relevant and retailer-ready. The big shift was how they treated post-launch.

2. **Risk-based approach.** We triaged the product portfolio using enforcement logic, not industry gossip. What were the highest-risk components? Which claims might trigger legal scrutiny? Which countries were most aggressive with enforcement? Every product was given a tailored risk profile. Materials in direct contact with the body had documented biocompatibility checks. Packaging with sexual wellness claims had evidence files linked directly to EU advertising standards, and any electronic SKUs had CE compliance properly substantiated, not just slapped on the box. This wasn't about perfection, it was about being bulletproof where it counted most.

3. **Compliance culture.** This wasn't siloed to one person or a dusty shared folder. The founder got involved. The sourcing lead started asking the right questions. The marketing team reviewed every claim for substantiation and flagged risk items before they made it to print. Most importantly, we set them up on VIGIL, our PMS tool. Customer complaints and feedback (as per ISO 3533) and adverse event trends all fed back into live records in any one of twenty-eight languages. If something changed in the market, the system caught it early.

The result: Armed with technical files, test reports, clear declarations and a post-market plan, Pulse & Bloom re-approached the same retail buyers that had stalled them before. This time, the answer was different. Legal sign-off was instant, buyers gave the green light and within three months, they'd secured shelf space with three multinational retailers, including one of the biggest pharmacy chains in Europe. They didn't just look compliant, they were de-risked, auditable and ready to scale.

Final word

Most brands in this space are winging it, but Pulse & Bloom didn't. They built compliance into their foundation, not because they had to but because they knew it would open doors. That's the ARC methodology advantage – not just protection but positioning.

The next five years will separate the operators from the optimists. The founders who treat compliance as strategy will thrive. Those who treat it as admin will stall, or worse. You get to choose which one you are, right now.

14

Creating Your Compliance Ecosystem For Scale

You've worked through core compliance, mapped your maturity and seen how the ARC methodology locks into your operations. You've probably also realised something uncomfortable: compliance is never finished. It lives, it breathes, it evolves with your business, and that means it needs routines.

It is essential to establish an ecosystem of processes and tools to support your regulatory obligations. Implementing your agile systems, a risk-based approach and a robust compliance culture will create a solid foundation for growth. By now, it should be clear: compliance is not a one-off project, it is a business discipline.

Creating your compliance ecosystem for scale

Five compliance routines to implement and create a habit

The following five routines are the heartbeat of a compliance-led, scalable, founder-proof business. This is where knowledge becomes rhythm. This is how founders stop firefighting and start leading.

1. Daily compliance power hour

This is the founder's firewall against chaos. It is not admin or box-ticking but a protected, non-negotiable, forward-looking block of time.

The mission

Spend one hour a day (or at least three times a week) not reacting to problems but building the systems that prevent them.

In this hour, you should:

- Review new regulatory updates in your sectors
- Check MAVRYX (or other document management systems) for outstanding tasks, gaps or expiring documents
- Interrogate recent customer complaints – is there a pattern emerging?
- Review open risk items from your risk register
- Audit a technical file: pick one product, open it, check it and find the weak spots before someone else does
- Work on strengthening PMS processes with your team
- Refine labelling checklists or update internal SOPs

Why this matters

If you only touch compliance when there's a fire, you're running a fire brigade, not a business.

The Daily Compliance Power Hour flips that. This is how founders stay in control.

2. Weekly risk and readiness review

This is the compliance equivalent of checking your bank balance. Every week, 30 minutes, no excuses. This is a simple pulse check to ask: Are we safe or are we running blind somewhere?

The mission

In this weekly review, you should check the following:

- Are any certificates, declarations or lab tests about to expire?

- Are any new SKUs waiting on documentation before launch?

- Have there been any supplier changes that impact technical files?

- Has anything triggered new risk, customer complaints, product returns or regulatory updates?

- Are you still within the bounds of your ARC risk register thresholds?

Treat it like a cash flow forecast but for risk.

Why this matters

Most brands only notice risk when it becomes a crisis. This routine means nothing sneaks up on you. It keeps invisible risks visible before they become expensive problems.

3. Monthly expert check-in

Compliance is a team sport. Whether you have an internal compliance lead, an external consultant or you're running it solo, you need a sounding board because you cannot see your own blind spots.

The mission

During this session you should:

- Run a sanity check on regulatory interpretations
- Validate decisions like market expansion, claim approvals or packaging changes
- Check progress on action items from your risk register or PMS logs
- Pressure test your next moves: 'Can we launch in Spain with this file?' or 'Are we clean enough for a marketplace audit?'

Why this matters

Founders do not get points for guessing right. You do not need to know everything, you need to build the habit of asking the right questions and getting the right answers before you move. Founders who do this avoid 90 per cent of avoidable compliance disasters.

4. Quarterly ecosystem reset

What worked last quarter might not work now. Every three months, step back from the day-to-day and ask: 'Is the system still fit for purpose?'

The mission

In this check, you should ask:

- Have regulations changed in any of your markets?

- Have new SKUs, formulations, components or supply chains introduced new risks?

- Have we hired new team members who need training on compliance processes?

- Are our SOPs still accurate or are we operating on ghost processes that nobody follows?

- Have any open risks aged out without action? That's a red flag.

- Are regulators starting to clamp down in a specific area? Is it time to pre-empt it? Look at enforcement trends in your industry.

Why this matters

Scale creates complexity. Complexity without a system becomes chaos. Chaos attracts enforcement. Quarterly resets are how grown-up brands stay clean, sharp and operationally safe.

5. Annual compliance growth plan

This is where compliance meets strategy. Once a year, before planning the next growth phase, compliance has to be part of the conversation.

The mission

At the annual compliance growth plan, you should ask:

- Are we expanding into new markets? What new obligations come with that?

- Are we onboarding new products, suppliers or third-party manufacturers? Have they been vetted?

- What investments are needed in systems, software, staff and consultants to match the next level of scale?

- Is our RP or AR structure still correct for where we trade?

- Do we need new testing, updated certifications or regulatory notifications?

- What's the game plan for enforcement risk next year: proactive audits, self-checks or marketplace file reviews?

Why this matters

Founders who show investors a solid compliance growth plan win. Brands who ignore this end up hitting invisible walls, sudden delistings, fines and recalls, right when they are trying to scale or raise.

This routine stops compliance from being a blocker and turns it into a growth enabler.

Final word

These routines are not admin or bureaucracy, they are operational resilience, enforcement risk insurance and scale readiness. Founders must build the muscle or pay the price.

When founders shift compliance from a stressful, reactive mess to a regular, predictable rhythm, the entire business unlocks with less firefighting, faster launches, safer operations, happier investors and fewer regulator headaches.

This is the difference between running a business that survives and one that scales confidently – fully loaded, fully protected and built to last.

15
Compliance Principles For Disruptive Entrepreneurial Success

By this point, you've built the mindset, mapped your maturity and locked in the ARC framework. You understand how core compliance keeps the lights on and how the Enforcement Risk Radar tells you where the danger lies. Now it's about anchoring this mindset into something unshakeable: a personal code.

The founder's operating code for regulated markets

The following nine principles are not theories; they are battle-tested truths from founders who have survived, scaled and thrived in some of the most aggressive and tightly policed industries on the planet.

1. You already have a mountain of data

You have every certificate, lab report, adverse event log and label revision. This is not paperwork, this is *intellectual property* – the proof that your brand plays at a professional level.

Most founders treat it like admin; the smart ones weaponise it. A clean compliance file is the difference between getting delisted overnight or passing an audit in 24 hours. It's the difference between getting hammered by enforcement or sending a polite file that shuts the case down.

Stop treating your documentation like a cost. Start treating it like an asset.

2. You can't predict the future, but you can own the assets

Regulations shift, enforcement priorities flip, markets close overnight and new standards arrive without warning.

You cannot control that, but ask yourself:

- Do you own your technical files?
- Do you have instant access to your test reports?
- Is your risk register real, current and yours, not buried in a consultant's inbox?

If the answer is no, you are not in control of your business. Full stop.

3. Work to build regulatory assets

Revenue is oxygen but assets are wealth.

In regulated industries, the brands that survive are not the ones with the best influencer strategy or the flashiest sales funnel, it's the ones with bulletproof files, robust safety claims, documented risk assessments and systems that scale.

Compliance is not admin, it's not overhead – it's an asset class. It reduces future risk, increases the company valuation and makes the business more attractive to retailers, investors and acquirers.

You are not doing this for red tape. You are doing this because compliance equity is real.

4. Go where the demand is strong and the rules are clear

Grey markets are sexy until they are not.

Selling into places where rules are vague, enforcement is patchy or compliance feels optional might make you money fast but it also puts you on the regulator's speed dial.

Clarity is power. If the rules are clear, you can build systems. If demand is strong, you can scale confidently.

The most resilient brands are the ones who stop chasing loopholes and start building for the long term.

5. Be a key person of influence in a risk-averse industry

In regulated markets, credibility beats creativity every time.

The founder who shows up publicly – who talks about product quality, consumer safety, testing and responsibility – becomes the brand people trust. You do not need to be boring or corporate, but you do need to be visible.

Post about your safety processes, show how you review products, share how you keep up with regulatory change. Retailers, investors, consumers and regulators notice. The loudest person in the room wins when they also happen to be the safest.

6. The market wants entrepreneurs who care about safety

Disruption without responsibility is dead.

Consumers and retailers are not stupid. Regulators are definitely not stupid. The world does not need another cheap product dumped into the market without care, safety or accountability.

The winners are the brands who combine innovation, speed, edge and accountability. If you care about safety, quality and consumer protection and you show it, you will outsell, outlast and outpace the people who do not.

7. You can't do it alone

Solo compliance is a death sentence. The landscape moves too fast. The rules are too fragmented. No founder – no matter how smart they are – can carry this alone.

You need:

- Systems like MAVRYX, SCOUT, VIGIL and VISTA

- Consultants who can translate legal into operational

- Staff who understand that compliance is part of their job, not just yours

If compliance lives in your head, it dies when you sleep. Build the ecosystem, share the load, scale the responsibility.

8. Success is driven by how much you care

Compliance is not deadweight. It is not a sunk cost. It is a contract with the customer, the retailer and the market itself.

Compliance is proof of care for consumer safety, for product quality and for long-term trust. The market rewards it: retailers open more doors; consumers come back; and investors pay higher multiples for clean, defensible businesses.

Trust compounds. Risk erodes value.

9. Compliance leaders are made, not born

Nobody is born knowing how to write a risk assessment or fluent in EU product safety law. You learn this, you build the muscle, you step up.

Every founder who has ever scaled a brand in a regulated industry started exactly where you are: overwhelmed, confused, winging it. The difference is, the ones who win decided to lead anyway. They asked questions, they built systems, they hired help, they took it seriously.

Leadership is a choice, and compliance leadership is one of the most valuable forms of it in the modern world.

Final word

These are not motivational slogans, this is the code that keeps founders safe, businesses clean and brands scaling without collapse.

When the pressure hits, enforcement, growth, recalls and investor scrutiny holds. This is the backbone. This is the edge.

Print it, frame it, tattoo it if you must. This is how the pros play.

16
CORE And ARC Methodology 90-Day Roadmap

This is not a theory exercise or paperwork for paperwork's sake. This is the operational playbook for turning compliance from a stressful, reactive time bomb into a scalable, founder-proof business discipline – one that protects your brand, accelerates growth and attracts retailers, investors and customers who care about trust.

CORE compliance

The CORE – Control, Observe, React and Establish – framework gives you structure:

- **Control.** How to stop and take stock of your situation.

- **Observe.** How you deep dive into the current status.

- **React.** How you begin creating the strategy for improvement.

- **Establish.** This guarantees you can prove what you claim, when it counts.

Together, these four checks take compliance out of theory and put it into practice.

The 90-day roadmap

You can move your business from chaos to control in just three months by using the following framework.

Days 1–30: Compliance clarity and quick wins

This is the stabilisation phase. You are not building perfection or optimising systems. Instead you are stopping the bleeding, surfacing the blind spots and creating a clear picture of what's broken, what's missing and what's working. Get clear, get safe, get the basics locked.

Key actions

- **Complete the ARC Scorecard.** Get a baseline maturity score across agile systems, risk and culture.

- **Run a compliance needs analysis.** Product by product, label by label, file by file, with no guesswork.

- **Appoint or confirm your compliance owner.** Whether that's an internal lead, an outsourced partner or you for now, someone owns it. Compliance without ownership fails.

- **Build your compliance asset library.** Use a tool like VISTA or a well-structured shared drive. No more 'searching inboxes for that certificate'. This is the foundation of all agility.

- **Fix urgent risks.** Gaps in technical files, missing RP appointments and broken labels – get them stabilised, fast.

- **Book your first expert check-in.** Bring someone in to reality-check your findings, assumptions and blind spots.

- **Surface your highest risks.** What could take you off the market tomorrow? What would cause a recall? This becomes your week one priority list.

The mission

- You are leaving reactive chaos behind.
- You are stepping into visibility, ownership and momentum.

Days 31–60: Systemise and strengthen

Build repeatable systems, remove single points of failure. This is the foundation-building phase, in which you are moving from scrambling to stability, from heroics to systems, from 'I think it's fine' to 'The system runs it, not me'.

Key actions

- **Build your document control and SOPs.** This is not bureaucracy, this is survival. Use the CORE principle: Observe.

- **Begin team training.** Everyone who touches product, packaging, marketing, sourcing or customer service needs to understand their compliance responsibilities. This is the ARC pillar: Culture.

- **Load, review and clean up your existing files.** Garbage in = garbage out. The library only works if the data inside it is accurate.

- **Set up weekly risk reviews.** Not optional: every week someone scans the horizon, expiries, gaps, supplier changes and new risks. Assign task ownership.

- **Build or refine your adverse event/customer complaint process.** This is where most brands fall over. Complaints are data; data is risk intelligence.

- **Apply the ARC lens to one product line.** Test how your new systems handle real-world conditions. Label review, risk assessment, PMS – stress test the process.

The mission

- You are no longer reliant on memory, inboxes or best guesses.
- You are building the compliance operating system that scales as you do.

Days 61–90: Scale and sustain

Build momentum, operationalise maturity, lock in the edge. This is where compliance stops being defensive and starts being a growth engine.

Key actions

- **Finalise your annual compliance growth plan.** Align it with commercial plans, new SKUs, new markets and new partnerships. Compliance now scales alongside revenue.

- **Create a compliance calendar.** This runs your year: audits, testing deadlines, RP renewals, PMS reviews, regulatory shifts. Everyone sees it and works to it.

- **Lock in your quarterly ARC ecosystem reviews.** Compliance is now a board-level function. It is tracked, discussed and improved just like finance, marketing or ops.

- **Build your risk-based product launch checklists.** From now on, nothing goes live until compliance clears it. Not after, not during – before.

- **Refine your PMS system.** Complaints flow into risk reviews, risk reviews update the system, and the business learns and adapts in real time.

- **Use the compliance maturity arc to score improvements.** Celebrate them, report them to investors and use them to unlock bigger retail contracts.

The mission

- Compliance is no longer a constraint, it is a competitive edge.

- It becomes a living, breathing, scalable operating discipline.

Final word

By following the CORE and ARC Methodology 90-Day Roadmap, at day 90 you will know exactly where you stand, what's missing and what's been fixed. You will have an active, functioning compliance operating system and your team will have rhythm, ownership and visibility.

You will be ready to scale: more SKUs, more markets and more growth, without collapsing under the weight of enforcement risk, paperwork chaos or regulatory blind spots.

You will have a founder story that makes retailers, investors and even regulators think: 'These are the people who take this seriously. These are the people we trust.'

17

How To Win Your First Audit

For most founders, the word 'audit' triggers the same fight-or-flight response as 'tax investigation' or 'regulatory notice'. You picture someone storming in with a clipboard, arms folded, dead-eyed, ready to tear your business apart. Trick questions, long silences, red pens poised for failure – it feels like an exam where you never got the syllabus.

Here's the truth founders rarely hear: An audit is not a trap or a courtroom. It is not designed to destroy your business. It is an opportunity, a chance to prove your operation is credible, competent and built for the long haul. Done right, it can strengthen your brand, elevate your reputation and open doors you didn't even know existed.

From panic to power: Turning scrutiny into strategy

The key? Preparation. With the right approach, you can turn fear into confidence and an audit into your competitive advantage.

Step 1: Know what type of audit you are facing

Not all audits are created equal. Some are quick checks, some are deep dives, some are collaborative, while others can feel confrontational. You cannot win a game you don't understand.

Start by asking:

- Who is auditing us? (Retailer, regulator, notified body, customs or a key supply chain partner)

- What is the scope? (One product, an entire market or company-wide systems)

- What are they looking for? (Documentation, product samples, SOPs or end-to-end processes)

- What's the time frame or focus area?

The sooner you understand the audit's parameters, the sooner you can stop guessing and start preparing strategically.

Step 2: Make your technical files audit-proof

This is the audit's backbone. If your technical files are incomplete, disorganised or scattered across inboxes, you're vulnerable.

At a minimum, you should be able to instantly produce:

- Full technical files for every SKU under audit

- Test reports, safety assessments and certifications

- RP agreements (if applicable)

- Label reviews, translations and packaging proofs

- Declarations of Conformity or equivalent market approvals

If you're running MAVRYX, VIGIL or any other structured document system, this is when it pays for itself. No inbox hunting, no 'which version was the latest?' panic, no missing certificates. Just clean, traceable, bulletproof evidence, on demand.

Auditors love speed and clarity. A founder who can produce a full, up-to-date technical file in under two minutes sets the tone for the entire audit.

Step 3: Prepare your people, not just your paperwork

Most founders think audits are about documents, but here's the catch: Auditors also audit your culture.

They ask questions like:

- Who is responsible for compliance?
- How does the customer service team handle complaints?
- What happens when a supplier changes materials?
- How are label updates tracked and approved?

Your team doesn't need to have the perfect answers, but they do need to understand their roles, know where the key documents live and be confident in how to escalate issues. Auditors aren't looking for superheroes, they're looking for proof that your business isn't flying blind.

Hold a 30-minute team prep session before the audit to walk through likely questions. Make sure everyone knows who speaks for what – nervous staff can sink a great technical file.

Step 4: Set the tone from the start

When the audit begins, you have a golden window to shape how it unfolds.

Be the leader. Open with:

- A summary of your compliance structure
- The systems you use to maintain readiness
- How the ARC methodology underpins your workflows
- Evidence of active risk management and PMS

This isn't about showing off, it's about signalling competence.

Auditors are human. They are reading you as much as they are reading your paperwork. Confidence, disorganisation and openness are signals – set the signal intentionally.

Defensive, flustered founders set off alarm bells. Calm, prepared founders make the audit feel like a box-ticking exercise.

Step 5: Follow up like a pro

Even the best-prepared brands sometimes get flagged for minor gaps. That's not the issue. What matters is how you respond.

If the audit identifies weaknesses:

- Stay calm
- Clarify expectations

- Document every action point

- Agree on deadlines before the auditor leaves

Then execute:

- Send missing documents promptly.

- Provide evidence of corrective actions.

- Tighten systems where needed.

The follow-up phase can be the difference between a warning and a clean sign-off.

The fastest way to tank an audit? Ignore the findings.

The fastest way to turn a shaky audit into a win? Fix it, fast, visibly and thoroughly.

The founder mindset shift

An audit is not an attack, it is a growth milestone, a credibility checkpoint, a trust-building exercise.

When you pass, you unlock:

- Bigger retailers

- Faster onboarding to marketplaces

- Investor confidence during due diligence

- Supply chain leverage with manufacturers and distributors

- Market expansion without legal chaos

This is not just about surviving scrutiny, it's about proving you can operate at scale.

Final word

Winning your first audit isn't about being perfect. No brand is perfect. It's about being:

- **Prepared.** Your documents are where they should be.

- **Proactive.** Your team knows what to expect.

- **Organised.** Your systems run without heroic effort.

- **Coachable.** You adapt quickly when gaps appear.

An audit isn't just a hoop to jump through. It's proof to the world, regulators, retailers and investors that you are not just another brand, you are an operator – a founder who plays the long game.

With the right systems, the right preparation and the right mindset, an audit stops being a threat and becomes one more way you win.

18

Compliance Red Flags And How To Fix Them Fast

If you are reading this, chances are you are asking yourself the same question that keeps most founders in regulated industries awake at night: 'Is my compliance house actually in order or am I just hoping for the best?'

Maybe your technical files are half-finished. Maybe your labels look fine but have never been properly risk-checked for different markets. Perhaps you are expanding into new territories and silently crossing your fingers that nothing gets flagged at the border by a retailer, or worst case by an enforcement body.

If this feels familiar, take a breath. You are not alone. Every founder building in a regulated market hits this moment. The key is not to panic but to spot the red flags early, take fast and decisive action, and prevent small issues from turning into brand-killing crises.

Here is the truth: You do not need to fix everything overnight but you do need to know where the danger zones are, what to do about them and act before the regulator, retailer or customer forces your hand.

Common compliance red flags and their fast fixes

Here we look at the problems along with the solutions that will take you from vulnerable to vigilant in one focused sprint.

Red flag 1: No centralised documentation

The problem

Your files are scattered across Google Drive, Dropbox, email threads, WhatsApp chats and random desktop folders. Nobody knows which version is current.

When someone asks for a certificate, it turns into a two-hour inbox search. Even then, you're not sure it's the right one.

The risk

You cannot pass an audit. You cannot onboard major retailers. You will fail a regulatory spot check.

The fast fix

Centralise your technical documentation now. Use a system like MAVRYX or – at a minimum – create a clearly structured cloud folder with:

- Version control

- Access permissions

- Assigned document owners

Rule: If it is not in the system, it does not exist.

This single move can take your compliance from 'we *think* we're covered' to 'we *know* we're covered'.

Red flag 2: Labels that have never been risk-checked

The problem

Labels are created by marketing or design teams with zero compliance input.

Everyone assumes they are fine because nobody has complained (yet).

The risk

Mislabelled products are one of the top causes of enforcement action.

Incorrect claims, missing icons or wrong translations can get you pulled from shelves, fined or publicly named on enforcement databases like the EU Safety Gate (RAPEX).

The fast fix

Run every label through a packaging compliance review.

Use a tool like SCOUT or a manual checklist to check for:

- Missing mandatory statements
- Unsubstantiated claims
- Incorrect translations or languages
- Wrong symbols, batch codes or warnings

Remember: A label is not just design. It is a legal document.

Red flag 3: No adverse event or complaint tracking

The problem

Complaints come in via email, Instagram DMs or calls to customer service... and then what?

No system, no tracker, just crossed fingers and hope.

The risk

Ignored complaints turn into investigations.

A single safety issue that is not logged or actioned can escalate into a recall, a fine, or worse, legal action from injured consumers.

Regulators ask for complaint logs. If you do not have them, you look negligent even if you are not.

The fast fix

Set up a simple PMS tracker. Whether it is a spreadsheet, a Google form or a tool like VIGIL, start logging:

- Date of complaint
- Product or batch affected
- Description of the issue
- Action taken
- Resolution and outcome

This alone can save you from being blindsided by enforcement.

Red flag 4: No formal compliance ownership

The problem

Compliance 'sits' with... whoever has time that week. No one owns it; everyone assumes someone else is handling it.

The risk

When everyone owns it, no one owns it. Tasks, label reviews, document updates and risk assessments fall through the cracks.

During an audit or due diligence, the question 'Who handles compliance here?' is met with blank stares.

The fast fix

Appoint a compliance lead. It does not matter if it is part-time, full-time or outsourced, but someone must have authority.

Give them:

- Clear responsibility

- Access to tools and resources

- Time in their role to manage it

Compliance without ownership is not just a risk, it is a ticking time bomb.

Red flag 5: Missing or expired certificates

The problem

You cannot find the Declaration of Conformity for your top-selling SKU.

The lab report on file is from 2019.

Your CE mark certificate expired last year... and no one noticed.

The risk

You cannot legally sell in certain markets.

Retailers can delist your products.

Regulators can block shipments, issue fines or force a recall.

The fast fix

Run a compliance audit of your top products:

- Check Declarations of Conformity.

- Verify test certificates and lab reports are current.

- Confirm RP appointments, where required.

- Flag anything that needs immediate retesting or renewal.

You cannot trade on expired compliance. Period.

Final word

Compliance red flags are a gift. Finding a red flag does not mean you failed; it means you caught it before someone else did. Regulators, retailers, competitors and consumers will find your red flags if you do not.

You do not need to panic, you do not need to be perfect, but you do need to be proactive.

These fast fixes will not solve everything, but they will buy you time, reduce your exposure and build confidence in your brand. They send out a powerful signal to investors, partners and retailers: 'This is a serious, defensible business, not a duct-taped start-up running on luck.'

Compliance is not a judgement, it is a journey. The brands who win are not the ones who avoid every mistake, they are the ones who see the warning signs and fix them fast.

Conclusion

If you've made it this far, you're not like most founders.

Most founders see compliance as an obstacle – something to tolerate, outsource, postpone or fudge their way through until they get caught – but not you. You picked up this book because you're building something bigger. Something credible that lasts. Something that doesn't crumble the first time a retailer asks for your technical file, a regulator shows up or a competitor challenges your claims. You understand that in today's world – where consumers are sceptical, regulators are watching and enforcement is getting sharper by the day – compliance isn't optional. It's your edge.

This book hasn't been about red tape, it's been about power. About showing bold founders in regulated industries how to turn compliance from a burden into leverage. From something you fear into something you wield. We've dismantled the myth that regulation is the enemy of growth. In its place, you now have a blueprint for action, backed by systems, tools and real-world experience.

Lessons we can take away

Let's pause and take stock. Let's remind ourselves what you've built in your hands so far and what to do next.

You have reframed compliance as a strategic advantage

From the very first chapter, we challenged the traditional view of compliance.

Compliance is not a dead weight or a necessary evil. It is not about avoiding fines or keeping regulators off your back. It's a business enabler, it's what gets you listed, it's what keeps you selling. It builds trust with retailers, regulators and customers and protects your long-term growth from the chaos that destroys less-prepared brands.

When you shift your perspective and see compliance as a strategic advantage instead of an administrative chore, your entire business transforms. You move faster, win bigger and build with certainty instead of hope. This shift in mindset is where real operational maturity begins.

You adopted the ARC mindset

We introduced the ARC methodology: agile systems, risk-based approach and compliance culture. This wasn't just theory, this was a lens through which you could assess your current position, identify weak spots and plot a path to maturity.

Agility gives you the flexibility to respond to change, whether that's a regulatory update, a supply chain disruption or a retailer onboarding demand.

Risk-based thinking helps you make smarter decisions, focusing your limited resources where they matter most instead of getting lost in busywork.

Culture ensures compliance isn't a one-person job. It becomes a living, breathing part of your company DNA, embedded in the way your team thinks and acts every single day.

This is not about chasing perfection, it's about knowing what 'good' looks like and building towards it with intention. Founders who embrace ARC are not just compliant, they're future-proof.

You worked through CORE compliance

The CORE framework gave you structure: Control, Observe, React and Establish. They take compliance out of theory and put it into practice.

You now know how to bring compliance to life across your products, teams and regions, and do it in a way that scales.

You learned how to build a scalable compliance ecosystem

Compliance is not a one-time project or a box to tick and forget, it's a system that grows as your business grows.

You now understand the importance of rhythm. From daily power hours to weekly risk reviews, monthly check-ins, quarterly resets and annual planning, you've seen how these routines transform compliance from a chaotic scramble into a steady operational heartbeat. The five routines don't slow you down, they keep you moving forward, faster, smoother and with more control.

Founders who adopt this rhythm stop firefighting and start leading.

You discovered the nine principles for founders in regulated markets

These principles are more than good advice, they are filters for how you operate, think and make decisions as a founder.

You now know:

- Your compliance systems and documentation are assets, not overheads.

- Trust is earned through evidence, not words.

- Defensibility isn't optional, it's your superpower in regulated markets.

When you live by these principles, you don't just build a safer business, you build a stronger, more credible, more investable one.

You recognised compliance as an investable asset

Compliance isn't just about avoiding trouble, it's about increasing valuation. You've seen how structured documentation, operational systems and audit-ready files make your business irresistible to investors and buyers.

Risk mitigation does more than protect. It enhances the value of your intellectual property. It signals to the market that you're not just another brand trying to get lucky, you're a professional operator, running a business built to scale.

This is what investor-ready compliance looks like. It accelerates deals. It increases multiples. It changes the game.

You were given the tools to act

You've learned how to:

- Spot red flags before they explode into crises

- Prepare for your first audit and turn it into a credibility builder

- Move from chaos to control with systems like MAVRYX, SCOUT and VISTA

- Build a risk register that actually gets used

- Create a culture where compliance isn't a blocker, it's part of the flow

The tools are in your hands. The question now is: What will you do with them?

What comes next?

You take the first step. Don't get overwhelmed – you do not need to implement everything all at once.

Start with your ARC Scorecard. Pick one routine and embed it. Review your top-selling product against the CORE compliance methodology. Block out time to build your annual compliance growth plan.

You are not behind, you are building with intention and if you want to move faster, the Arcus team is here. Whether it's strategic support, compliance helpdesk solutions or fully managed systems, you are no longer alone in this journey.

The most exciting industries in the world are also the most scrutinised. That's where the biggest opportunities lie.

The founders who win are not the ones who dodge regulation, they're the ones who master it. They use compliance as a growth engine. They sleep at night knowing the foundations are solid. They operate with credibility, confidence and control. They earn the right to lead.

Final word

This is your moment – build boldly, operate responsibly, lead with credibility.

Stay bold, stay compliant, keep your edge.

The world doesn't need more founders who play small. It needs founders like you – willing to do the hard, smart, necessary work to build brands that last. This is how you scale without fear. This is how you create value that compounds.

This is how you win.

Glossary

Adverse event: Any negative incident or reaction linked to a product after it has been placed on the market. Tracking these is part of PMS and is legally required in most regulated sectors.

Agile systems (ARC Pillar): Compliance systems that can respond quickly to regulatory change, new product development or market expansion. This includes version-controlled documentation, modular SOPs and real-time updates.

ARC methodology: A strategic framework made up of three pillars: agile systems, risk-based approach and compliance culture. Designed to help founders scale compliance with clarity and control.

Audit: A formal review or inspection of your documentation, processes or systems by a regulator, retailer, notified body or internal team. Being audit-ready means your files are complete, organised and up to date.

Authorised Representative (AR) (EU)/Responsible Person (RP) (UK): A legally appointed person or entity that acts on behalf of a non-EU or non-UK manufacturer to ensure compliance and market access. They may also be the first point of contact for market surveillance authorities.

Compliance culture (ARC Pillar): The behaviours, attitudes and habits within your team that ensure compliance is not just one person's job, it is a shared responsibility embedded in day-to-day operations.

CORE compliance framework: A practical tool made up of four pillars – Control, Observe, React and Establish – that helps founders structure and implement compliance at any stage of growth.

Declaration of Conformity (DoC): A formal document stating that a product meets all applicable regulatory requirements. Usually signed by the manufacturer or their appointed representative.

Due diligence: An investigative process conducted by investors, buyers or partners to assess the legal, financial and operational readiness of your business – including compliance documentation.

Evidence: The data, reports, certificates and records that prove your product meets legal and safety requirements. Without evidence, claims cannot be substantiated.

Label review: The process of checking product labels against regulatory standards. This includes ingredients listings, mandatory warnings, translations, claims and country-specific formats.

MAVRYX: An Arcus Compliance document management and compliance platform. It supports structured file storage, version control, packaging reviews and post-market tracking, all in one system.

Post-market surveillance (PMS): The ongoing process of monitoring a product after launch to identify and address any risks, defects or user issues. Required in sectors like medical devices, cosmetics and vapes.

Product Information File (PIF): A core compliance document required for cosmetics in the UK and EU. It includes formulation data, safety assessment, manufacturing details and labelling information.

Responsible Person (RP): A role required in the UK and EU for products like cosmetics, vapes and medical devices. The RP ensures legal compliance, maintains documentation and acts as a contact for authorities.

Risk-based approach (ARC Pillar): Allocating your compliance resources based on the level of risk. High-risk products or markets get more scrutiny and documentation, while lower-risk areas are streamlined.

SCOUT: An Arcus Compliance automated packaging and label review tool. Helps ensure your product packaging meets local legal requirements before going to market.

SCPN/CPNP: The UK and EU notification portals for cosmetics. Products must be registered here before they are legally sold.

Technical file: A collection of documents that demonstrate your product meets regulatory requirements. Includes risk assessments, test reports, declarations and manufacturing records.

VIGIL: An Arcus Compliance PMS tool that tracks complaints, adverse events and incidents. Helps brands stay compliant after launch and feeds real-world data back into risk management.

VISTA: An Arcus Compliance digital system for document version control and workflow automation. Supports agility by helping teams manage files, sign-offs and updates with confidence.

Acknowledgements

The acknowledgements section is always the hardest to write – not because there aren't enough people to thank but because there are too many. Every part of this book – every lesson, every story, every scar – has someone's fingerprints on it.

To my mum, Linda, you've been my constant. Every ounce of fight, honesty and stubborn belief that runs through me started with you.

To my son, Freddie, you're the reason I push harder, stay up later and dream bigger. Everything I build is ultimately for you.

Most recently, to Gemma, thank you for opening my eyes to something new. Your support and love have been a quiet revolution.

To everyone who's walked the Arcus journey with me. From those first clients who believed in what we were doing before we even had a name to the incredible team who've helped turn an idea into something real: John Walker, Keelie Turnbull, Sebastian Wisniewski, John Donoghue, Hannah Fury, Robert Sidebottom and all the staff who've come and gone but left their mark, you've all helped shape what Arcus Compliance has become.

To the friends, mentors and thinkers who inspired this book and the mavericks who taught me that rebellion and responsibility can co-exist, thank you for showing me that doing good and doing well don't have to be opposites.

Finally, to the clients, collaborators and even the critics, thank you. You've all contributed to the conversations that made this book worth writing.

This book isn't really mine, it's ours.

The Author

Lee Bryan is the founder and CEO of **Arcus Compliance**, a company that helps brand owners in regulated industries turn compliance from a burden into a competitive advantage. Since 2017, he has guided some of the world's most recognisable brands across novel nicotine, cosmetics, consumer electronics, PPE, adult toys and children's toys through complex UK and EU regulations.

Motivated by losing family members to smoking-related illnesses, Lee made it his mission to protect consumers and champion purpose-driven entrepreneurs who want to do things right. His first book, *How Safe Is Your Vape?*, became an Amazon #1 bestseller and established him as one of the most trusted voices in the compliance space.

With *The Compliance Edge*, Lee turns his focus to the next generation of founders – the mavericks disrupting the status quo. The book is designed for those without six-figure compliance budgets but with the drive to build safer, stronger, and more ethical brands. It furnishes these challengers with the insight, tools, and mindset to punch up and stand toe to toe with multinationals, proving that doing the right thing can also be a powerful competitive edge.

in www.linkedin.com/in/leejohnbryan

www.ingramcontent.com/pod-product-compliance
Lightning Source LLC
Chambersburg PA
CBHW011933190326
41519CB00029B/7504